SOCIAL CAPITAL

Social capital has become a core theoretical concept in the Social Sciences – linking deep insights from sociology and political theory to eminently practical applied interventions within communities and organizations. With this book, Dr Singh provides a clear, cogent review of the current state of the field and how researchers and policymakers can leverage social capital for deep, positive social change. The scholarship is thorough and insightful, tracing the roots of the idea and linking it with modern digital developments and applications across multiple policy domains. This book deserves a place on the shelf of anyone engaged in development research, practice, and policy making.

                                                       – Prof James Moody, *USA*

SOCIAL CAPITAL

Evolution, Contestation, Application and Digitization

BY

MUDIT KUMAR SINGH

Duke University, USA
Jaypee University Anoopshahr, Bulandshahr,
Uttar Pradesh, India

emerald
PUBLISHING

United Kingdom – North America – Japan – India
Malaysia – China

Emerald Publishing Limited
Emerald Publishing, Floor 5, Northspring, 21-23 Wellington Street, Leeds LS1 4DL

First edition 2024

Copyright © 2024 Mudit Kumar Singh.
Published under exclusive licence by Emerald Publishing Limited.

British Library Cataloguing in Publication Data
A catalogue record for this book is available from the British Library

ISBN: 978-1-83797-588-4 (Print)
ISBN: 978-1-83797-587-7 (Online)
ISBN: 978-1-83797-589-1 (Epub)

Printed and bound by CPI Group (UK) Ltd, Croydon, CR0 4YY

INVESTOR IN PEOPLE

To my toddler daughter

.

CONTENTS

LIST OF FIGURES, TABLES AND BOXES

Appendix

Chapter 4

ABSTRACT

Do we really know social capital? Moreover, is our understanding of the 100-year-old term is consistent with the digital world? This book delves into the intricacies of social capital, examining its historical evolution, contemporary contestation, and practical applications. The author introduces a novel refurbished notion of social capital that will improve our conceptual and practical understanding about the term while outlaying future course of actions.

This book begins with an in-depth analysis of the evolution of social capital, tracing its roots from early little known nonscientific casual use (1905) to its modern-day conceptualization. It explores the different concepts, dimensions, and application of social capital, including bonding, bridging, and linking social capital; and how these knowledge contours have changed over time in the digital era. The author examines how social capital has evolved from the traditional society to the age of social media, and online communities. The work describes how social capital is shaped up by social relationships, norms, and institutions and how it also has influenced them in due course of time. It critically examines the confused and ambiguous use of social capital in measurement and conceptualization by scholars, practitioners, and policymakers.

One of the key focuses of the book is the evolution and contestation of social capital term over the years and across the disciplines while recognizing digital form of social capital in present time. It critically examines the debates and controversies surrounding social capital, including issues of inequality, power dynamics, and social exclusion. After a thorough examination, the author devises a sound understanding of the term that has originated in writings of the early scholars while criticizing the ambiguous and overlapping usage that emerged over time in scholarly debates and practice. The author traces the early debates and tensions within and that between sociologists and economists that distorted the meaning of social capital, and made the term highly ambiguous and complex. Not only the concept but also its forms, and states of being of the term has been varying even in the most popular works that the author will bring fore to the discussion.

On a positive note, this book will examine how social capital has been used for positive social change, including its role in civic engagement in citizen support groups in the United Kingdom, community development programs in Latin America, Africa, and South Asia, and economic welfare in the United States and European countries. The author highlights successful examples of social capital application in the digital realm, ranging from crowdsourcing initiatives to social entrepreneurship, and provides practical recommendations for leveraging social capital for social good in the digital era. While briefly introducing the darker side of social capital in the digital era, such as the spread of misinformation, echo chambers, and online polarization, the author discusses the ethical and moral implications of social capital in a rapidly changing digital landscape. This book is a thought-provoking and timely exploration of the multifaceted concept of social capital in the context of the digital revolution. The write-up has offered a comprehensive overview of the evolution of social capital, critically examines its contestation in the digital age, and provides practical insights for harnessing social capital for positive social change.

FOREWORD

Dr Mudit Singh is a social scientist with PhD from Motilal Nehru Institute of Technology, Allahabad. As a postdoctoral scholar, he worked in sociology discipline of Humanities and Social Sciences Department of Indian Institute of Technology, Kanpur. He worked on the problem of democratic participation in Panchayati Raj Institutions (PRI). He has published a framework on Participatory Local Governance of Energy Transition. The framework was successfully presented before the Elke Weber team at Princeton and other international and national forums. He combines the spirit of a fieldworker and a theorist of social capital. He has published a book, several papers and research reports on social issues and development interventions.

In this book, the author delves into the transformation of social capital from its traditional roots to its modern manifestations in the age of social media and online communities. The text explores how social capital is intricately shaped by social relationships, norms, and institutional structures, while also shedding light on its reciprocal influence on these very elements over time. This book takes a critical stance on the often perplexing and ambiguous utilization of the concept of social capital, a phenomenon observed across the scholarly, practical, and policymaking realms. Central to the book's focus is the historical evolution and ongoing debates regarding the term "social capital," acknowledging its digital adaptation in today's world. The author conducts a thorough examination of these debates and controversies, which encompass issues of inequality, power dynamics, and social exclusion. Ultimately, the author strives to offer a more coherent and well-founded understanding of a concept that was originally rooted in early scholarship but became entangled in an intricate web of overlapping and uncertain usage throughout the course of scholarly discourse and practice.

Furthermore, this book sheds light on how social capital has been harnessed for positive societal transformation, highlighting its role in various contexts such as citizen support groups in the United Kingdom, community development programs across Latin America, Africa, and South Asia, and its contribution to economic welfare in the United States and European nations. While briefly acknowledging the potential negative aspects of social capital in the digital era, such as the dissemination of misinformation, the creation of echo chambers, and the exacerbation of online polarization, the author also delves into the ethical and moral considerations tied to social capital within the swiftly evolving digital landscape.

In sum, this book serves as a thought-provoking and timely exploration of the multifaceted concept of social capital in the context of the digital revolution, offering a comprehensive review of its evolution, a critical examination of its contested nature in the digital age, and practical insights for harnessing social capital for positive societal progress.

I think the students and young scholars of sociology, development studies, civil society action, and program implementation would benefit significantly from this book.

Arun Kumar Sharma
Senior Professor of Sociology (Retd)
Indian Institute of Technology Kanpur
16 October 2023
Kanpur

FOREWORD

Social capital has impacted billions of lives since its inception and is equally popular among academicians and policymakers. The term has been applied by the international agencies such as the World Bank and the United Nations since last three decades.

Social capital has been used for positive social change, including its role in civic engagement in citizen support groups in the United Kingdom, community development programs in Latin America, Africa, and South Asia, and economic welfare in the United States and European countries. This book by Dr Mudit Kumar Singh introduces a novel refurbished notion of social capital that will improve our conceptual and practical understanding about the term in the digital era. The book is a thought-provoking and timely exploration of the multifaceted concept of social capital in the context of the digital revolution. The write-up has offered a comprehensive overview of the evolution of social capital, critically examines its contestation in the digital age, and provides practical insights for harnessing social capital for positive social change. The author highlights successful examples of social capital application in the digital realm, ranging from crowdsourcing initiatives to social entrepreneurship, and provides practical recommendations for leveraging social capital for social good in the digital era. While briefly introducing the darker side of social capital in the digital era, such as the spread of misinformation, echo chambers, and online polarization, the author discusses the ethical and moral implications of social capital in a rapidly changing digital landscape.

Chapters in the book will cater to the needs policymakers and that of UG and PG students from wide discipline including Computer Science, Management, Sociology, and Political Science.

I wish Dr Singh's contribution to the knowledge of social capital will benefit the society around the globe.

(Prof Dr V P Kallimani)
VC, Jaypee University Anoopshahr
PhD, Nottingham University
7 December 2023

ACKNOWLEDGMENT

My heartfelt thanks to Professor James Moody, Duke Network Analysis Center, Duke University, for his continued support in my academic pursuits. I thank Prof (Retd.) Arun Kumar Sharma, Indian Institute of Technology, Kanpur, and Dr Jessica Streib, Associate Professor, Department of Sociology, Duke University for my orientation in social capital and contemporary social problems. I thank Dr Jaemin Lee (now Assistant Professor, Chinese University, Hong Kong) for contributing to my working group on social capital during my visit to the United States in 2018 sponsored by Fulbright-Nehru Doctoral Fellowship. I am thankful to the Postdoctoral Fellowship at Just Transition Research Centre, Department of Humanities and Social Sciences, Indian Institute of Technology, Kanpur, for the conducive academic environment to write the book proposal in early stages. I extend my thanks to the two anonymous reviewers, serene, fraternity of Jaypee University Anoopshahr and to the entire Emerald editorial team for the smooth process of review and revisions.

1

ORIGIN AND CONCEPT OF SOCIAL CAPITAL

The term "social capital" was first introduced by L. J. Hanifan in his 1916 publication titled "The Rural School Community Center." In this publication, Hanifan defined social capital as follows:

> ...those tangible substances [that] count for most in the daily lives of people: namely good will, fellowship, sympathy, and social intercourse among the individuals and families who make up a social unit... [Social capital] accrues to the individual and to society by virtue of the social contacts which are established in the community... (Hanifan, 1916, p. 130)

Social capital is a multidimensional concept that encompasses various forms of social connections, networks, and norms that shape social interactions within a community or society. The concept was popularized by sociologists in the 1980s and 1990s, and it has since gained significant attention from scholars across various disciplines, including political science, economics, and public health. Social capital has been recognized as a valuable resource that can have a significant impact on various aspects of individuals' lives, including their economic, social, and mental well-being. However, social capital is not a homogeneous concept; it can take on different forms that can have varying implications for individuals and communities.

THEORETICAL FRAMEWORKS AND APPROACHES TO UNDERSTAND SOCIAL CAPITAL

Social Network Approach

This framework emphasizes the structure and characteristics of social networks and how they facilitate the creation, maintenance, and utilization of social capital. It focuses on the patterns of social ties, such as the strength, density, and diversity of social networks and how they shape the flow of resources and information among individuals and groups.

Social capital is embedded in the structure and composition of social networks, including the size, density, diversity, and strength of ties among individuals and groups (Granovetter, 1973).

Social capital, defined as "the resources embedded within social networks that individuals and groups can access and utilize" (Lin, 2001, p. 22), has been widely studied from the perspective of social network theory. Social network theory posits that social networks play a crucial role in the development and distribution of social capital (Burt, 1992; Granovetter, 1973). According to Burt (1992), the position of individuals within a social network, such as their centrality and connectivity, determines their access to social capital. Granovetter (1973) argued that the strength of social ties, such as trust and reciprocity, influences the formation and distribution of social capital. Furthermore, cognitive processes, such as individuals' perceptions of their social networks, also shape their access to social capital (Nahapiet & Ghoshal, 1998).

Empirical research has provided evidence supporting the social network theory of social capital. For instance, studies have shown that social networks and social capital are positively associated with individual well-being. For example, individuals with larger and more diverse social networks tend to have higher levels of subjective well-being and life satisfaction (Putnam, 2000). Social networks also play a role in economic outcomes, as they provide access to job information, resources, and opportunities (Burt, 1997). In addition, social networks and social capital have been linked to better health outcomes, including improved mental health and reduced mortality rates (Kawachi & Berkman, 2001).

However, there are also critiques of the social network theory of social capital. Some scholars argue that social network theory tends to focus on individual-level factors and may not adequately capture broader structural and contextual factors that influence social capital (Portes, 1998). Others raise concerns about the potential for social capital to exacerbate inequalities, as social networks and social capital can be exclusive and unequally distributed, leading to the concentration of resources in certain groups (Brulle & Pellow, 2006).

The social network theory of social capital provides a valuable framework for understanding how social networks contribute to the formation and distribution of social capital. Empirical research has supported the role of social networks in shaping individual and societal outcomes. However, further research is needed to better understand the complex interplay between social networks, social capital, and broader social structures and to address potential inequalities in the distribution of social capital.

Trust, Norms and Values

This framework highlights the importance of trust in fostering social capital. Trust is seen as a crucial element that enables individuals to rely on one another, cooperate, and engage in collective actions. Trust can be built through repeated interactions, shared norms, and common values, and it serves as a foundation for social capital formation and functioning.

The theory suggests that social capital is built upon the foundation of trust, which enables individuals to engage in cooperative behaviors, exchange resources, and establish social connections (Putnam, 2000). Trust is recognized as a crucial element in the concept of social capital, which refers to the resources embedded within social networks that individuals and groups can access and utilize (Coleman, 1988; Putnam, 2000). Trust is often viewed as a foundational component of social capital, as it facilitates cooperation, collaboration, and exchange among network members (Burt, 2005; Fukuyama, 1995). Trust can be defined as the expectation that others will behave in a reliable and cooperative manner, based on shared norms, values, and experiences (Mayer et al., 1995).

Theories on trust in social capital have evolved over time. One of the prominent theories is the social exchange theory, which posits that trust emerges from repeated interactions and exchanges among network members, where individuals learn to rely on others' trustworthiness through past experiences of reciprocal behavior (Blau, 1964; Cook & Emerson, 1978). According to social exchange theory, trust is built through a process of repeated interactions and the development of shared expectations of reciprocity, leading to the formation of social capital.

Norms are shared expectations and rules that guide individuals' behavior, and values are deeply held beliefs and principles that influence social interactions. Norms and values can shape social capital by influencing social cohesion, cooperation, and collective action in a community or society.

Institutional Theory

This framework focuses on the role of formal and informal institutions in shaping social capital. Formal institutions include laws, regulations, and formal organizations, while informal institutions include norms, customs, and traditions. Institutions can influence the formation, maintenance, and utilization of social capital by providing the structure, rules, and resources for social interactions and cooperation. Brehm and Rahn (1997) argue that "the institutional context plays a critical role in shaping social capital at the individual level". They provide evidence on how formal and informal institutions influence the formation and consequences of social capital, particularly in the context of political participation (Brehm & Rahn, 1997, p. 999). Woolcock (1998) proposes a theoretical synthesis and policy framework for understanding the relationship between social capital and economic development. He argues that "the institutional context, including formal and informal institutions, shapes the creation and utilization of social capital, and influences its impact on economic development". Portes (1998) emphasizes the role of institutional arrangements in shaping the distribution and consequences of social capital in communities. He argues that "formal and informal institutions influence the availability, accessibility, and mobilization of social capital, which in turn affects various outcomes, such as economic development, social integration, and civic participation". Putnam (2000) explores the role of institutions in the decline of social capital in American society. He argues that "changes in formal institutions, such as the decline of civic organizations and social norms, have contributed to the erosion of social capital in the United States" (Putnam, 2000, p. 19). Fukuyama (2001) discusses how institutions shape the formation and consequences of social capital at the societal level. He argues that "the quality of institutions, such as the rule of law, property rights, and governance structures, affects the development and utilization of social capital, which in turn influences economic and social outcomes" (Fukuyama, 2001, p. 47). Woolcock and Narayan (2000) emphasize the role of institutions in shaping the relationship between social capital and development outcomes in different contexts. They argue that "institutions, both formal and informal, mediate the relationship between social capital and development, and contextual factors shape the formation, maintenance, and utilization of social capital" (Woolcock & Narayan, 2000, p. 235). Schneider et al. (1997) examines how institutional arrangements influence the distribution and consequences of social capital in different societies. They argues that institutional factors, such as legal frameworks, cultural norms, and social hierarchies, shape the formation, distribution, and utilization of social capital, and influence its impact on various outcomes, such as economic development, civic engagement, and social cohesion.

Human Capital Theory

This framework emphasizes the role of individual skills, knowledge, and education in fostering social capital. Human capital refers to the attributes and capacities of individuals that can be invested in social interactions and relationships. Individuals with higher levels of education, skills, and knowledge are often more likely to participate in social networks, engage in collective actions, and access social resources, thereby fostering social capital.

Human capital theory suggests that individuals with higher levels of education, skills, and knowledge are more likely to engage in social interactions, participate in social networks, and foster social capital (Coleman, 1988).

Coleman (1988) emphasized the role of individual human capital, such as education, skills, and knowledge, in the formation and utilization of social capital. Coleman argues that "individuals with higher levels of human capital are more likely to participate in social networks, establish trust, and engage in collective action, which can result in greater social capital" (Coleman, 1988, p. S95). Bourdieu argues that "cultural capital influences the types of social networks and relationships individuals can access, which in turn affects the amount and quality of social capital they can accumulate" (Bourdieu, 1986, p. 241). Bourdieu (1986) extends the human capital theory of social capital by emphasizing the importance of cultural capital, which includes education, values, and norms, in the formation and distribution of social capital. Lin (2001) further develops the human capital theory of social capital by highlighting the role of cognitive skills, such as problem-solving and communication abilities, in the formation and utilization of social capital. Lin argues that individuals with higher cognitive skills are more likely to effectively utilize social networks, establish trust, and engage in collective action, which can enhance social capital. Portes and Sensenbrenner (1993) emphasize the role of human capital in shaping the development of social capital among immigrant communities. They argue that "education, skills, and language proficiency are important forms of human capital that influence the formation and utilization of social capital among immigrants, which can have implications for their integration and well-being in the receiving society" (Portes & Sensenbrenner, 1993, p. 132).

Human capital theorists argue that "education, as a form of human capital, positively influences the formation of social networks, trust, and participation, which can contribute to the accumulation of social capital" (Flap & Völker, 2001). Uslaner (2002) examines the role of education in the formation of social capital, particularly in the context of political participation. Uslaner (2002) argues that "education is an important form of human capital that can enhance political knowledge, participation, and engagement, which can result in greater social capital." Sabatini and Sarracino (2017) extends the human capital theory of social capital by exploring the role of education and skills in shaping social capital in the digital era. Sabatini argues that "digital literacy, online communication skills, and the ability to navigate social media platforms are emerging forms of human capital that can influence the formation and utilization of social capital in the digital age." Table 1 summarizes the literature review of social capital without considering digital implication on the term.

Evolution of Social Capital Over the Years

The concept of social capital has evolved over the past 100 years with a very gradual speed until scholars in the United States and Europe popularized the concept by linking it with the social phenomena of policy importance. The popularity of the term "social capital" can be gauged by the fact that there are as many as 89,500 documents on Google scholar database that contain the phrase in their title itself. Similarly, Web of science shows 12,448 documents on conducting the search for "social capital". Just to illustrate the knowledge contours built around the term, I will discuss the social capital evolution across the disciplines, countries over the years according to Scopus database. The key word search criteria "Social Capital" yielded 35,356 documents ranging from 1936 to 2024 listed on Scopus. I filtered down the documents to 2022 for better representation and authenticity with time. The years 1936 and 1968 had one document each and are included in the analysis. The final analysis consists of 34,519 documents. Since the search criteria is almost all inclusive and includes reports, peer reviewed papers, books, and conference proceedings, there is less likely a chance that the search will exclude any important

Table 1. Some Social Capital Concepts by Known Authors.

Conceptualizing Social Capital	Authors
Social capital is the aggregate of the actual or potential resources that are linked to possession of a durable network of more or less institutionalized relationships of mutual acquaintance or recognition.	Bourdieu (1986)
Social capital can be defined as (1) a source of social control, (2) a source of family-mediated benefits, and (3) a source of resources mediated by nonfamily network.	Portes (1998)
Social capital encompasses the features of social organization, such as trust, norms, and networks, that can improve the efficiency of society by facilitating coordinated actions.	Putnam (2000)
Social capital is the social resources that individuals and groups possess through their networks of relationships, including social ties, shared norms, and values.	Lin (2001)
Social capital is a resource for action. It consists of the networks of relationships among people, including their levels of trust, reciprocity, and cooperation.	Coleman (1988)
Social capital is the social interconnectedness, trust, and cooperation that exist within and between individuals and groups.	Kawachi et al. (2004)
Social capital refers to the social networks, norms, and trust that facilitate collective action and cooperation among individuals and groups.	Woolcock and Narayan (2000)
Social capital is the social resources and social ties that individuals and groups can access, which can result in beneficial outcomes.	Nahapiet and Ghoshal (1998)
Social capital concept is poorly specified and the use of the term is inherently problematic, and needs to be carefully critiqued and empirically grounded before it can usefully be applied in social policy formulations.	Morrow (1999)
Social capital encompasses the social relationships, networks, and norms that create social cohesion and facilitate cooperation and collaboration.	Uslaner (2002)
Social capital is the social connectivity, mutual support, and shared values that contribute to community development and well-being.	Fukuyama (1995)

document, and although a few of the uncategorized documents (0.97%) are left from the analysis, it will help readers to build an understanding about social capital term in the literature. Fig. 1 suggests there are only a handful documents traceable in Scopus database until 1988. But we see a sharp takeoff post-2000 as the term was widely applied to numerous public policy programs and used heavily by researchers from social science and management disciplines alike.

'Documents' over the 'Years'

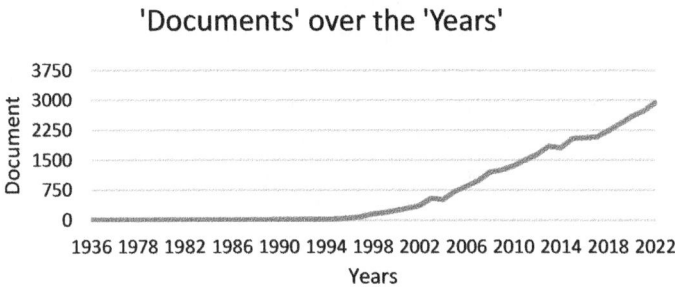

Fig. 1. Social Capital Literature Growth According to Scopus Database.

Documents by Subject Area

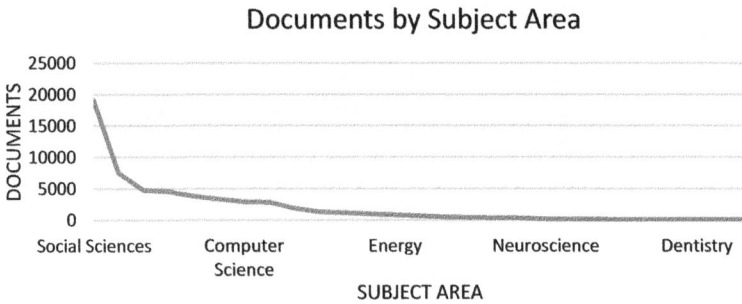

Fig. 2. Discipline Wise Documents in Social Capital.

Fig. 2 shows discipline wise distribution of social capital usage gives us an idea how social capital gained its wide presence across multiple disciplines from natural to social sciences and humanities. Conforming to its origin in 1916 and later usage of the term by social scientists, there is a huge amount of work from the disciplines of social sciences that goes to other natural science disciplines.

2

FORMS OF SOCIAL CAPITAL

In the first chapter, we saw social capital has been recognized as a valuable resource that can have a significant impact on various aspects of individuals' lives, including their economic, social, and well-being. However, social capital is not a homogeneous concept; it can take on different forms that can have varying implications for individuals and communities.

To start off this chapter, I will take two renowned early scholars of social capital who had a huge impact on understanding forms of social capital in early ages.

First, Bourdieu (1986) who did not explicitly discuss the forms of social capital, and second, Coleman (1988) who proposed three forms of social capital: obligation and expectation, information channel, and social norms.

Bourdieu discussed forms of capital but never explicitly discussed the forms of social capital as for him, social capital often exists in connection with other forms of capital (cultural and economic) that is based on individuals' *habitus*. After a careful review of his works, one can definitely identify his idea of social capital largely rooted in the networks that individuals make for reproduction and sustainability of social groups that can be less or more formalized (e.g., family, clubs, associations). By doing so, social groups take advantage of social capital concentrated in the groups. Though, it does not benefit all equally and leaders of the groups (e.g., trade union leader, kings of royal courts), get symbolic power in the name of their group. So, we could infer the existence of two forms – network form concentrated in groups and symbolic form that people use to achieve power and social status that maintains the social structure.

For Coleman, three forms of social capital are generated due to the functioning of social capital in individual relations that is conditioned by the social structures. For an instance, the vital information about trades is held secretly by individuals connected within the particular trade, and hence, it can be a form of social capital. Likewise, obligation and expectation arise out of a mutually benefiting relation between two individuals – obligation for one and expectation by the other with no legal compulsion to fulfill either. So, there may be outstanding credit slips of social capital if unfulfilled on either part.

Lastly, the third form is social norms. Is social norm really a form of social capital?

Scholars like Putnam and Lin discussed about other forms of social capital that were categorized more on the basis of different outcomes that social capital generates by the virtue of different nature of individual connections.

Beyond the academic pursuits, scholarly work sponsored by international agencies such as Asian Development Bank also acknowledged various forms of social capital in program interventions. Carroll (2001) has summarized multiple forms discussed by the early propounders of social capital into six categories: (1) family and kinship connections, (2) community networks, (3) cross-sectoral linkages, (4) institutional policy framework, (5) sociopolitical (state–civil society) relations, and (6) social norms and values. Mostly, network is a common thread in all the forms of social capital that reflects connection between social actors (family or organization).

While these forms indicate that connections are the essential requirement for social capital, the social capital exists in multiple levels of our social structure. These structures are not always clearly segregated and may overlap; however, assuming a stationary (for a certain time) form of social capital aggregated in social groups, we can broadly identify three levels where social capital may exist in our social structure – micro, mesh, and macro. There often exist common threads across these structures, and it is not always easy to draw hard line boundaries as these are social structures and evolve over the base of other structures. Yet, by bringing the administrative level into the context, especially in formal social structures, one can identify these three broad classes of social capital.

MICROLEVEL

Microlevel social structures are the building blocks of larger societies. They include individual relationships, family units, kinship networks, and small community-level groups. These structures are the intimate, day-to-day contexts in which people interact, learn, and develop their identities. Let's explore the roles and functions of these microlevel social structures in manifesting and reproducing culture and norms.

INDIVIDUAL RELATIONSHIPS

At the most fundamental level, individual relationships contribute to the transmission and reinforcement of cultural norms and values. People form connections with friends, colleagues, and acquaintances who share similar beliefs and practices. Through these relationships, individuals learn about and internalize societal norms, behaviors, and values. For example, if an individual consistently interacts with peers who prioritize environmental sustainability, they are more likely to adopt similar values and behaviors over time.

Moreover, individual relationships can serve as bridges between different cultural groups. In multicultural societies, individuals who have diverse social networks can facilitate the exchange of cultural practices and promote tolerance and understanding. These interactions can help mitigate cultural misunderstandings and conflicts.

FAMILY UNITS

Families are perhaps the most influential microlevel social structures in shaping cultural norms and values. Families are where individuals first learn about social roles, responsibilities, and moral principles. The transmission of cultural heritage occurs through generations within the family unit.

Family dynamics, rituals, and traditions all contribute to the perpetuation of cultural norms. For example, religious practices and celebrations are often observed within family settings, passing down spiritual beliefs and customs to younger members. Additionally, the way families communicate, express emotions, and resolve conflicts greatly influences how individuals interact with others and understand societal expectations.

KINSHIP NETWORKS

Kinship networks extend beyond the immediate family and encompass a broader web of relatives, including cousins, aunts, uncles, and grandparents.

These networks provide a sense of belonging and identity that is deeply rooted in cultural traditions. Kinship ties often involve mutual support, both emotional and material, which strengthens social bonds and reinforces cultural norms.

In many societies, kinship networks play essential roles in rites of passage, such as weddings and funerals. These events serve as opportunities to reaffirm cultural practices and values, as they involve the participation of a wide range of relatives who collectively uphold and pass on these traditions. Kinship networks also facilitate the exchange of knowledge, stories, and historical narratives that are integral to cultural preservation.

LOCAL-LEVEL GROUPS

Community groups, like youth clubs in villages or staff clubs in universities or small towns, represent microlevel social structures that bring individuals together with shared interests or affiliations. These groups create spaces for socialization, collaboration, and the reinforcement of cultural norms.

Youth clubs, for instance, often serve as platforms for young people to engage in activities that reflect their cultural heritage. They may organize cultural festivals, dances, or storytelling sessions that celebrate local traditions. Through participation in these activities, young club members learn about their cultural roots and develop a sense of pride in their heritage.

Staff clubs in universities or small towns can also foster a sense of community and shared identity among their members. These clubs often organize events, sports activities, and cultural exhibitions that promote cultural exchange and understanding. By doing so, they contribute to the broader social fabric by fostering an environment where diverse cultural backgrounds are respected and celebrated.

The groups manifest and reproduce the culture and norms of the groups by virtue of the social capital they hold in the close connections. Individual, family, kinship, and small community-level groups (a youth club in a village, staff club in a university or small town) are examples of microlevel social structures that hold social capital in their networks.

MESO (INTERMEDIATE) LEVEL

Intermediate-level social structures are unique community aggregations shaped primarily by external legal and political factors. These structures serve as bridges between local communities and higher administrative levels, both within national and subnational contexts. Examples of such structures include trade unions, associations, and clubs, which gather individuals with common interests or goals. These entities often cluster or federate groups from various local communities, forming district-level aggregations that expand their reach while maintaining a connection to grassroots concerns.

One distinct characteristic of these intermediate-level social structures is their ability to establish connections with cross-sectoral power holders within the broader social system. This trait enables them to advocate for local communities effectively and access resources and opportunities that might be otherwise challenging to attain.

These intermediate-level structures are essential in amplifying the voices of local communities. They provide a platform for individuals and smaller community-based groups to make their concerns known and advocate for their interests. This connection to grassroots issues is a significant strength of these structures, as they possess a deep understanding of local needs.

One illustrative example of the influence of intermediate-level social structures is found in federations of women in resource-poor countries. These federations typically represent women from diverse local communities who face various challenges, such as economic hardship and gender inequality. Through their district-level aggregation, these federations consolidate their influence and become significant players in the broader social system.

One way in which these intermediate-level structures wield their influence is by establishing connections with politicians. Politicians recognize the potential voting bloc represented by these structures and may seek their support in elections. In exchange, politicians often pledge to champion the interests of these groups, both in terms of policy initiatives and resource allocation. This illustrates the capacity of intermediate-level structures to leverage their collective power to influence political decision-making.

A practical benefit of these political connections is increased access to government-sponsored schemes and programs. By aligning with politicians who support their cause, federations of women can gain insights into available government resources and schemes that can address the specific needs of their communities. This access can translate into improved living conditions, economic opportunities, and social services for the women they represent.

Another significant role played by these intermediate-level structures is in facilitating economic development. For instance, the clustering of women's groups from multiple villages to pursue potential business ventures can be made possible through these structures. By pooling resources, expertise, and market access from various local communities, these clusters can create sustainable businesses with a more significant impact.

The significance of intermediate-level social structures is evident in their capacity to bridge the gap between local communities and the broader social system. They serve as conduits for information, resources, and opportunities that would otherwise be challenging for isolated local groups to access. This is particularly vital in resource-poor and marginalized communities, where challenges are multifaceted, and collective action is crucial.

Through their connections with politicians and government agencies, these structures can bring about tangible improvements in the lives of community members. These improvements may include increased access to education, health care, economic opportunities, and social services. In this way, intermediate-level social structures act as powerful agents of change in resource-poor and marginalized communities.

In conclusion, intermediate-level social structures are pivotal in fostering connections between local communities and higher administrative levels. These structures, such as trade unions, associations, and district-level aggregations, provide a platform for advocating local concerns, accessing resources, and forging connections with cross-sectoral power holders. Their ability to establish political connections, advocate for local communities, and facilitate economic development underscores their importance in amplifying the voices of marginalized and resource-poor communities.

MACROLEVEL

Often, there are aggregated forms of mesostructures at international, national, and subnational levels. International and national associations of lawyers, academicians, labors, etc., all are examples of macro level social capital that are subjected to complex political and legal forces. Social capital in these types of structures are often influenced by the individual authority on the positions, e.g., secretary, president, etc. These may be indirect or direct representation of mass or select group of people. Elected state governments, intergovernmental organizations, and other regional associations formed for economic development are examples of this category of social capital that has its roots in community groups who elect their representatives, and in many cases, these representatives elect representatives at higher levels. This process of direct and indirect election or selection holds true in all the democratic forms of formation of large institutions that are often little away from the direct connection of people at the microlevel. In many cases, these macro groups get influenced and regulated by the law and political power.

In later chapters, we will see how these forms are often confused with other fundamental concepts leading to over stretching of the term and contributing to its "confused" variability. As we learned, there exist multiple threads across the three structures discussed above; we can say the social capital must be formed and influenced by the individuals in these structures. In the following section of this chapter, we will explore these connecting forms of social capital, including bonding, bridging, linking, and lastly, digital capital.

BONDING SOCIAL CAPITAL

Bonding social capital, as conceptualized by Putnam (2000), refers to the cohesive ties and close relationships that develop within homogenous groups, such as family units, close friends, or members of the same cultural or ethnic community. This form of social capital is rooted in shared norms, values, and identities, fostering a sense of trust, reciprocity, and mutual support among individuals who belong to the same group. The dynamics of bonding social capital can provide social support, enable collective action, and cultivate a distinct sense of belonging and identity within these tightly knit circles.

Within the framework of bonding social capital, close-knit families serve as quintessential examples. In family units, the bonds forged through bonding social capital offer more than just emotional connection; they provide practical assistance during times of crisis and challenges. This might entail offering support, sharing caregiving responsibilities, or providing financial aid. Moreover, the bonds of trust and loyalty among family members contribute to a stable and supportive environment. This type of social capital not only strengthens the family unit but also reinforces the shared values and norms that guide the interactions within it (Lin, 1999). Bonding social capital can also contribute to the socialization of individuals into cultural or ethnic norms and values (Lin, 2001). For instance, within an ethnic community, bonding social capital can help individuals maintain their cultural heritage, language, and traditions through social interactions with others who share the same background (Portes, 1998).

Bonding social capital plays a pivotal role in shaping cultural and ethnic communities as well. Within such communities, individuals share a common heritage, language, and background. The bonds established through bonding social capital facilitate the preservation of cultural identity. This form of social capital helps individuals to uphold and pass down their traditions and values, ensuring the continuity of their cultural legacy. For instance, within an ethnic community, individuals can engage in social interactions with others who share their cultural background. These interactions not only provide a sense of familiarity but also serve as a means of transmitting cultural norms and practices to younger generations.

However, it is important to recognize that bonding social capital is not without its potential drawbacks and negative implications. One notable concern is the potential for social exclusiveness and the reinforcement of ethnic or cultural boundaries. As bonding social capital becomes more pronounced within a particular group, it can inadvertently create barriers that limit interactions and engagement with individuals outside of that group. This can lead to social fragmentation and exclusion, as those who do not belong to the group find it challenging to access the benefits of the close-knit social fabric.

An illustrative example of this dynamic can be observed in the context of immigrant communities. While bonding social capital helps immigrants maintain connections and support networks within their own ethnic or cultural group, it can simultaneously impede their integration into the wider society. Studies have shown that strong bonding social capital among immigrants can lead to social closure, where individuals primarily interact within their own community and have limited interactions with the broader society. This can hinder opportunities for social integration, economic mobility, and access to resources beyond the immediate community.

Bonding social capital is a powerful force that shapes close relationships within homogenous groups, whether they are family units, close friends, or members of cultural or ethnic communities. It fosters trust, mutual support, and a sense of identity among individuals who share common norms and values. However, while bonding social capital offers numerous benefits such as emotional support, cultural preservation, and a strong sense of belonging, it can also contribute to social exclusiveness and reinforce barriers between different groups. Recognizing the dual nature of bonding social capital is crucial for understanding its impacts and implications in diverse societal contexts. As communities navigate the complexities of social capital dynamics, striking a balance between maintaining strong internal bonds and promoting openness to external interactions becomes essential for fostering inclusive and cohesive societies.

BRIDGING SOCIAL CAPITAL

Bridging social capital refers to the weak ties and connections between different groups or communities (Putnam, 2000). Bridging social capital, a concept introduced by Granovetter (1973), encapsulates the significance of forging connections that traverse various social, cultural, and economic boundaries. Unlike bonding social capital that thrives within close-knit groups, bridging social capital emphasizes the establishment of diverse networks that extend beyond immediate circles. These networks can facilitate the flow of information, enhance social mobility, and provide access to resources that might otherwise remain untapped.

One of the defining features of bridging social capital is its potential to bridge gaps and overcome barriers. Granovetter (1973) argued that weak ties in diverse networks can offer unique advantages. These connections often expose individuals to novel information and perspectives that they might not encounter within their usual social circles. This is significant because diverse information flow through bridging social capital can lead to enhanced opportunities for personal and professional growth. For example, someone seeking a job might uncover potential employment opportunities by tapping into their broader network, which can include acquaintances from different fields or industries.

Furthermore, bridging social capital plays a crucial role in promoting social cohesion and fostering cooperation across diverse groups. As individuals interact with others who hold different backgrounds and viewpoints, they develop a broader understanding of society's complexities. This understanding can encourage collaboration and empathy, as people recognize the shared humanity that transcends superficial differences. Thus, bridging social capital contributes to the creation of a more inclusive and interconnected society, where people are more likely to work together for common goals.

Bridging social capital is also instrumental in expanding individuals' access to resources and opportunities. In the context of health services, for instance, individuals with diverse networks are more likely to be informed about available health care options and support services (Kawachi & Berkman, 2001). This access to information can lead to better health outcomes and well-being. Similarly, during times of need, individuals who possess strong bridging social capital may find themselves connected to a wide array of resources, ranging from financial assistance to emotional support.

The concept of bridging social capital aligns with Putnam's (2000) assertion that diverse networks can enhance social integration. By interacting with individuals from different backgrounds, people develop a broader understanding of society's complexities and challenges. This understanding can contribute to a more cohesive social fabric, where individuals are more likely to empathize with one another and collectively address issues that affect their community. Bridging social capital is thus a valuable asset in fostering a sense of shared responsibility and promoting social change.

Nonetheless, it is essential to acknowledge that building and maintaining bridging social capital can also present challenges. Establishing connections across diverse networks might require individuals to step out of their comfort zones and engage with unfamiliar groups. This can be particularly daunting for individuals who are naturally more introverted or who lack opportunities for exposure to different social circles. Additionally, the quality of weak ties within diverse networks can vary, and some connections might not yield substantial benefits in terms of information or resources.

Bridging social capital can also contribute to social integration and reduce social inequalities by promoting interactions and relationships between individuals from different backgrounds (Putnam, 2000). For instance, studies have shown that bridging social capital can foster social integration between different racial and ethnic groups, promote cross-cultural understanding, and reduce prejudice and discrimination (Lin, 1999). Bridging social capital can also foster social cohesion and civic engagement, as individuals with diverse networks may be more likely to engage in collective action for the common good (Putnam, 2000). However, bridging social capital can also face challenges, such as maintaining trust and reciprocity among diverse groups with different norms, values, and interests (Putnam, 2000). This can lead to a lack of social cohesion and cooperation, especially in diverse communities where there may be tensions or conflicts among different groups (Lin, 1999).

LINKING SOCIAL CAPITAL

Linking social capital can be understood as the connections and networks between individuals or groups and formal institutions, such as government agencies, nonprofit organizations, or businesses. Linking social capital involves individuals' ability to access and mobilize resources and opportunities through formal institutions and networks (Woolcock & Narayan, 2000). Linking social capital can facilitate access to social services, employment opportunities, and political participation (Woolcock & Sweetser, 2002). For example, individuals who have connections with strong government agencies or nonprofit organizations may have better access to public services, such as education, health care, or social welfare (Szreter & Woolcock, 2004).

Linking social capital can also contribute to social and economic development at the community and societal levels (Szreter & Woolcock, 2004). For instance, studies have shown that communities with strong linking social capital tend to have higher economic growth, better governance, and improved public health outcomes (Woolcock & Narayan, 2000). Linking social capital can also promote social and political participation, as individuals who have connections with formal institutions are more likely to engage in civic activities, such as voting, volunteering, or advocating for policy changes.

However, linking social capital can also face challenges, such as unequal access to formal institutions, especially for marginalized or disadvantaged groups (Woolcock & Narayan, 2000). For example, individuals from lower socioeconomic backgrounds, minority groups, or remote communities may face barriers in accessing formal institutions, such as language barriers, discrimination, or lack of resources. This can result in a normative bias where certain groups are excluded from the benefits of linking social capital, leading to social inequalities and marginalization.

Three key forms of social capital are often discussed: bonding, bridging, and linking. These forms operate at different levels of social interaction – micro, meso, and macro – each offering unique benefits and challenges. Critiques and supporters of social capital both applied their logic often from an isolated standpoint of their understanding.

The key is to use different frames of references when conceptualizing and applying social capital to the real-world social actors and contexts. Table 2 can help to understand the changing frame of reference from microlevel to macrolevel that coincides with bonding, bridging, and linking capital for an

Table 2. Three Forms of Social Capital at Different Levels.

	Bonding	Bridging	Linking
Micro	Family, close friends	Friends in two groups	Connection in government
Meso	Friends in same groups and neighbors	Friends in separate groups	Contacts between local associations and powerful people in government or other (e.g., lawyer) associations
Macro	Friends in associations (town clubs, unions)	Friends in two separate associations at similar levels (unions in same town in different company)	Connection between higher level representatives of social organizations (union leaders, lawyers associations at state/ national levels)

easier understanding of the social capita term and its applications in real-world situations.

At the microlevel, bonding social capital refers to the strong ties and connections individuals have with their immediate family and close friends. These relationships are characterized by high levels of trust, reciprocity, and emotional support. Within this close-knit circle, individuals often find a sense of belonging, security, and identity. For instance, a person's bond with their family can provide a safety net during times of crisis, while friendships offer companionship and emotional sustenance.

Bonding social capital is essential for personal well-being. It provides a support system that can boost mental and emotional health. When individuals face challenges or need assistance, their bonds with family and close friends serve as valuable resources. However, it can also have limitations, as it may lead to insularity and homogeneity, limiting exposure to diverse perspectives and opportunities outside one's immediate circle.

Moving to the meso level, bridging social capital involves connections with individuals who belong to different social groups or networks. These connections can include friends from separate social circles or interactions with neighbors. Bridging social capital fosters diversity and social cohesion by exposing individuals to a wider range of ideas, experiences, and worldviews.

Bridging connections can lead to the exchange of information and resources across different social groups. For example, someone with friends in various professional or interest-based groups may have access to a broader range of knowledge and opportunities. Neighbors who interact regularly can create a stronger sense of community and support systems within a neighborhood.

One of the key benefits of bridging social capital is the potential for innovation and creativity. Exposure to diverse perspectives and ideas can stimulate novel solutions to problems and promote social learning. However, maintaining these connections may require more effort and skill, as they involve managing relationships across different social contexts.

At the macrolevel, linking social capital extends beyond personal networks to encompass connections with institutions and powerful individuals in positions of authority. These connections are often vital for accessing resources, opportunities, and information on a broader societal scale. Examples of linking social capital include relationships with government officials, leaders of influential organizations, or members of professional associations.

Linking social capital can facilitate access to important resources, such as job opportunities, government services, or funding for community projects. For instance, an individual with connections in the government may find it easier to navigate bureaucratic processes and secure support for community initiatives. Similarly, a professional with ties to influential industry associations might gain access to valuable industry insights and networks.

However, linking social capital can also present challenges, particularly related to power imbalances and ethical considerations. The reliance on connections with influential individuals or institutions can lead to inequalities in resource distribution and reinforce existing power structures. Moreover, the ethical use of linking social capital is essential to avoid situations of nepotism or favoritism.

Bonding, bridging, and linking social capital operate at different levels of social interaction and offer distinct advantages and limitations. Bonding social capital provides essential emotional support and a sense of belonging within close-knit groups. Bridging social capital promotes diversity and social cohesion by connecting individuals across different social circles. Linking social capital facilitates access to resources and opportunities on a broader societal scale through connections with institutions and influential figures.

Balancing these forms of social capital is essential for individuals and societies. While bonding social capital is crucial for personal well-being, bridging and linking social capital contribute to social integration and access to resources. An ideal scenario involves a combination of these forms, allowing individuals and communities to thrive while fostering a more inclusive and equitable society. Understanding the interplay between these forms of social capital is vital for creating strong, resilient, and interconnected communities. While acknowledging the above strands of social capital literature, I bring perspectives of critiques of social capital into coming chapters. I then conclude by adding my own insights to a refurbished understanding of the term that may or may not conform to some of the connotations attached to the social capital.

DIGITAL SOCIAL CAPITAL

The evolution of digital social capital can be traced back to the early days of the internet, with the emergence of online communities and forums that provided spaces for people to connect, share information, and collaborate (Preece, 2000). These early forms of digital social capital were primarily focused on niche interests and hobbies and were limited to a relatively small group of users. However, with the rise of social media platforms, such as Facebook, Twitter, and Instagram, digital social capital has taken on new dimensions, becoming more widespread and accessible to a larger audience (Ellison et al., 2007).

The affordances of social media, such as the ability to create profiles, share content, and interact with others, have enabled the formation of digital social capital on a massive scale. Social media platforms have allowed individuals to connect with others who share similar interests, beliefs, or backgrounds and have facilitated the development of online communities and networks (Boyd & Ellison, 2008). These online connections have the potential to foster social capital by enabling the exchange of information, emotional support, and social resources (Valenzuela et al., 2009). I have used the terms digital capital and digital social capital interchangeably to denote the same meaning: interaction between social capital and technology.

THE RAPID GROWTH OF DIGITAL CAPITAL LITERATURE

Although there are sufficient reasons and conviction in recognizing the digital capital as a separate entity, the scholarly variation in its conceptualization and usage requires a reconfiguration of the term that may link its concept and usage. Especially, when measuring digital capital, scholars often lack a sound conceptual comparison with Bourdieusian capital and the digital capital (Ragnedda, 2018). Without much innovation in the term, scholars have used the digital capital extensively to explain civic participation in social media (Bimber, 1999; Bimber & Jorba, 2010; Gil de Zúñiga, 2012; Skoric et al., 2016). Economic view of resource utilization and profit making has long used the term digital capital in the context of investment in business setup to strengthen human capital (Liu, 2008b; Tapscott et al., 2000).

These contesting views and philosophies trigger the questions "What is digital capital?" Is it a tangible or intangible entity that people create and accumulate? More importantly, for policymaking and business settings, "how to operationalize digital capital for public welfare and profit making"?

For example, Fig. 3 indicates that the word growth trajectory in Scopus database is indicating a hyped growth rate in the last five years or so.

The country production in Fig. 4 suggests out of the total 102 documents, more than one-fourth (26%) production comes from the United Kingdom, China, and the United States. There are three countries from global south (India, South Africa, and Morocco) showing very limited contribution (only four) and indicating the reach of the research percolating from the European countries.

Similarly, Fig. 5 shows the collaborative production is dominated by Europe (the United Kingdom and Italy).

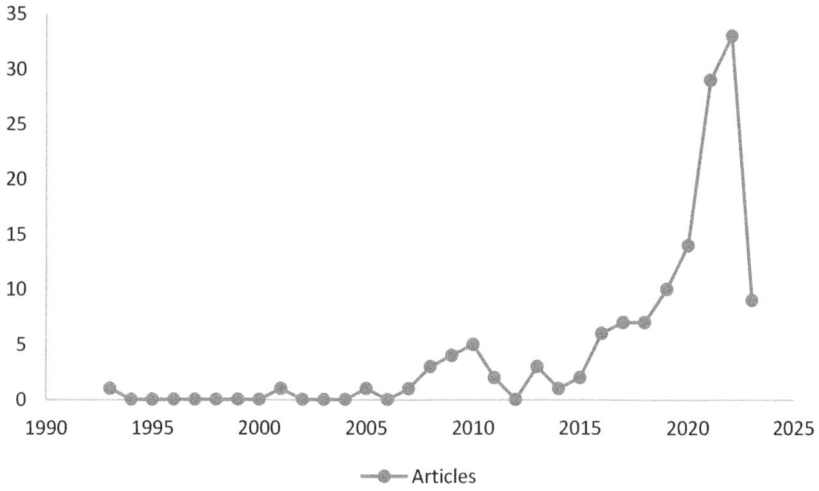

Fig. 3. Growth in Popularity of the Terms in Digital Capital Research.

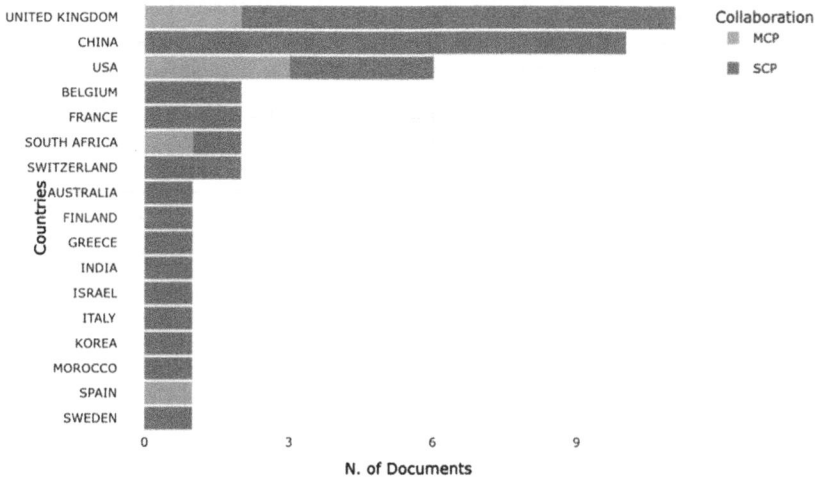

Fig. 4. Country Production (SCP: Single-Author Country Production, MCP: Multi-Authored Country Production).

IN-DEPTH REVIEW OF DIGITAL CAPITAL

In early stages, the term was popular in the business world without a direct influence of Bourdieusian concept of capital, and the idea was popular in the business world as an interaction of internet and investment (Liu, 2008a, 2008b; Tapscott et al., 2000). In the later phases, interaction between Bourdieusian form of capitals (social, economic, and cultural) and technology was

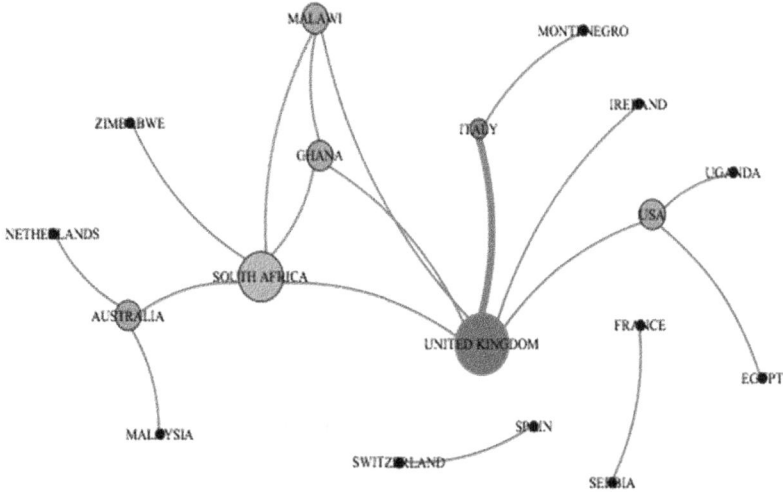

Fig. 5. Country Collaboration Network on Digital Capital Research.

treated as digital capital (Seale, 2013) that other scholars popularized as a more developed version of Bourdieusian capital (Ragnedda, 2018) and addressed more social (digital divide and sociotechnical inequality) angle of digital capital. On the other hand, scholars gave due attention to the business-oriented concept of digital capital that gave attention to a person's competency and access to infrastructure, enabling a person to access digital capital that endorse its investment oriented version of intangible capital (Bannykh, 2020; Bannykh & Kostina, 2022).

Table 3 summarizes the key concepts of digital capital used in the relevant literature.

Digital capital is a resource to develop new products and services (Bughin & Manyika, 2013). Likewise, scholarship convincingly argues to treating data from a capital perspective (economic capital) to understand better the impact of political–economic regimes (Sadowski, 2019). Some of the comprehensive work on defining digital capital builds upon (Bourdieu, 1986) notion of capital. He interprets the concept of capital as a resource that can be accumulated and perpetuated over time. More specifically, capital must be understood as a sum of resource that empowers social agents within specific fields. Bourdieu locates the social capital source into *more or less institutionalized connections* (Bourdieu, 1986). Thus, the origin of social and digital capital is similar in terms of their presence in the individual and institutional connections. The broader difference between the two is that the former originates in a natural social world while the other in a virtual world.

Table 3. Concepts of Digital Capital and Relevant Authors.

Conceptualization of Digital Capital	Author(s)
Digital capital is a new "Bourdieusian capital" that influences digital inequalities and measured as a specific capital.	Calderón Gómez (2021); Darcy et al. (2019); Ragnedda (2018); Ragnedda and Ruiu (2020)
Digital capital is the accumulation of digital competencies and digital technologies.	Bannykh and Kostina (2022)
Access to technology as a digital capital by university students separate from social and cultural capital that students posses.	Seale (2013)
Digital capital is the intangible assets gained through knowledge and relationships.	Liu (2008b)
Digital capital is an intangible form of capital created by firm-specific investments in information technology.	Tambe et al. (2020a, 2020b)
Digital capital is a four-dimensional concept measured through sum of internet customers, internet service, internet innovation, and internet relational capitals.	Liu (2008a)
Digital capital can be seen as access to technology through government-supported infrastructure and education.	Bannykh (2020)
Digital capital is a measure of internet usage that is shaped by technical capabilities and willingness to avail online services.	Tilleczek and Campbell (2019); Бородкина and Сибирев (2021)
Digital capital is a new form of capital that combines material and nonmaterial components.	Magomedov et al. (2020)
Digital capital is a combination of human, social, and symbolic capital tradable in various areas of one's life.	McGillivray and Mahon (2021)
Digital capital is the set of tangible and intangible digital assets and digital competencies of employees that increase labor productivity.	Merzlikina and Mogharbel (2022)
Digital capital is the communication system between enterprises and potential consumers in a virtual internet environment.	Spitsina et al. (2022)
Digital capital is a resource used to produce added value in almost all areas.	Bubnov et al. (2021)
Digital capital is an investment that creates an intangible form of capital.	Tambe et al. (2020a, 2020b)

(Continued)

Table 3. (*Continued*)

Conceptualization of Digital Capital	Author(s)
Digital capital is an investment by people (employers and contractors) in a business setup.	Tapscott et al. (2000)
Digital capital refers to the conditions that determine how people access, use, and engage with digital technology.	Park (2017)

Ignatow and Robinson (2017) also interpret capital as the socially valued scarce resources that can be transformed and reinvested. Social capital (Bourdieu, 1986) is one of the most widely used theoretical concepts applied to explain individual behavior across the disciplines of sociology, psychology, political science, and economics.

Hence, despite the fact that plenty of capitals are present in the social science discipline, a new form of capital requires a separate recognition as digital capital and should not be seen merely as a dimension of existing social capital (Ragnedda, 2018; Ragnedda & Ruiu, 2020).

Early social capital researchers (Dudwick et al., 2006; Grusky & Lin, 2019; Woolcock & Narayan, 2000) conceptualized social capital as a social entity operating based on individual covariates (age, education, race, occupation, and gender) and social affiliation (e.g., membership in a range of civic bodies). Many collective theorists emphasized trust and social norms as a conceptual base of social capital (Cook Lin & Burt, 2001).

Consequently, many social scientists use trust between individuals and institutions as a proxy to measure social capital. But these techniques and concepts require survey approaches that need resource investment. With many dimensions and some conceptual differences, by and large, scholars agree on a common ground that the trailing term capital indicates resource advantages of various kinds to the group members and individuals, enabling them to achieve worthwhile goals (Field, 2003; Singh & Lee, 2020).

Like Bourdieu's concept of field and *habitus*, the entire digital space can be seen as a field where social agents can position themselves or leverage their digital capital to their advantage (Ragnedda & Ruiu, 2020). The positions in the newly constructed digital field vary according to the social agents' access and level of competence. However, in doing so, they provide only a bridging concept and identify digital capital as another form of capital along with the others, viz. social, economic, cultural, political, personal, and digital (6 Cs).

Table 4. Comparing Social and Digital Capital.

Factors	Bourdieusian Capital	Digital Capital
Origin	Institutionalized connections: Embedded in social relations and structures	Internet: Digital devices using web services and apps that virtually connect individuals
Movement	Networks carry social capital between two connecting actors	Flow virtually through connected digital users and machines
Forms	Sense of belongingness, trust between actors of the society, collective groups	Sense of belonging to virtual communities, web pages, and social media groups
Distribution	Distributed across the social categories of connecting actors	Distributed across the individual's digital communities conditioned by the access and extent of using the technology
Measurement	Survey-based respondent-reported trust, membership in civic bodies, number of collective groups	Membership with the online community, communication, and usage pattern observable on a real-time basis
Externalities	Same as any other social science research	A high degree of conditioning of digital environment: Mediating and occasionally interfering

Table 4 summarizes the comparative frame of Bourdieusian capital and digital capital.

However, the evolution of digital social capital has not been without challenges and controversies. One of the key debates surrounding digital social capital is the quality versus quantity dilemma, with concerns about the depth and authenticity of online connections (Williams, 2006). Critics argue that digital social capital may be shallow and superficial, as online interactions often lack the nuances of face-to-face communication and may be prone to misinterpretation (Vitak, 2012). Additionally, issues of privacy, online harassment, and misinformation pose challenges to the development and maintenance of digital social capital, as they can erode trust and create negative experiences (Livingstone & Helsper, 2007).

Digital social capital has significant impacts on individuals, communities, and society as a whole. One of the key impacts of digital social capital is on individual well-being and mental health. Research has shown that digital social capital can have positive effects on individuals' mental health by providing social support, reducing loneliness, and fostering a sense of belonging (Kross et al., 2013; Valenzuela et al., 2014). Online interactions can also enhance individuals' self-esteem and self-worth, as they receive feedback, validation, and recognition from their online connections (Ellison et al., 2014).

Furthermore, digital social capital has implications for civic engagement and political participation. Social media platforms have been used as tools for political mobilization and activism, facilitating the exchange of information, opinions, and resources among like-minded individuals (Bimber et al., 2012). Digital social capital can also facilitate civic participation through online volunteering, crowdfunding, and community organizing efforts (Shah et al., 2005). However, it is important to note that digital social capital can also contribute to polarization, echo chambers, and the spread of misinformation, which can have negative impacts on democratic processes and societal cohesion.

Digital social capital also has implications for economic outcomes, particularly in the context of the gig economy and online marketplaces. Research has shown that digital social capital, such as positive online reviews, ratings, and recommendations, can impact individuals' trust and reputation, influencing their success in online transactions and economic exchanges (Resnick et al., 2013). Digital social capital can also facilitate access to job opportunities, information, and resources through online professional networks, which can have implications for individuals' career advancement and economic well-being (Ellison et al., 2014).

Digital social capital has become a significant concept in the contemporary digital age, shaping the way people connect, interact, and collaborate online. Its evolution, impacts, and implications have been the subject of extensive research and debate. While digital social capital has the potential to foster positive outcomes, such as individual well-being, civic engagement, and economic opportunities, it is not without challenges and critiques. Issues of social inequality, privacy, data exploitation, and misinformation pose challenges to the development and maintenance of digital social capital. However, digital social capital also has applications in various domains, including public health, disaster response, education, and entrepreneurship, indicating its versatility and potential for positive impact.

Digital social capital is a complex and multifaceted phenomenon that has both positive and negative aspects. As the digital landscape continues to evolve, it is important to recognize the role of digital social capital in shaping online interactions and relationships and its potential implications for various aspects of society, including democracy, economy, and well-being. Further research and discussions are needed to better understand the dynamics of digital social capital, its impacts, and ways to mitigate its challenges. Policy-makers, platforms, and users should strive to promote responsible and ethical use of digital social capital, ensuring that it benefits all individuals regardless of their social, economic, and demographic backgrounds.

In this way, we understood social capital as a multidimensional concept that encompasses different forms of social connections, networks, and norms that shape social interactions within a community or society. Bonding social capital refers to the strong ties and close relationships within homogenous groups; bridging social capital refers to the weak ties and connections between different groups; and linking social capital refers to the connections and net-works between individuals or groups and formal institutions. Digital social capital refers to the varied forms of social capital generated due to the inter-action of the three social capital types and digital technology.

Each form of social capital has its strengths and limitations, and it can have varying implications for individuals and communities.

Bonding social capital can provide social support, foster a sense of belonging and identity, and contribute to the socialization of individuals into cultural or ethnic norms and values. However, it can also lead to social exclusiveness and reinforce ethnic or cultural boundaries, perpetuating social inequality and exclusion of individuals who do not belong to the group. Bridging social capital can facilitate information flow, social mobility, and social integration, but it can also face challenges in maintaining trust and reciprocity among diverse groups. Linking social capital can facilitate access to resources and opportunities through formal institutions, promote social and economic development, and enhance civic participation. However, it can also face challenges in unequal access, leading to social inequalities and marginalization.

It is important to recognize that social capital is not a one-size-fits-all concept, and its implications can vary depending on the context and individ-uals involved. Scholars have also debated the bias of social capital, as different forms of social capital can have different effects on social inequalities and biases. For example, bonding social capital can reinforce existing social hier-archies and norms, while bridging and linking social capital can promote social integration and inclusion but may also exclude certain groups or perpetuate power imbalances (Putnam, 2000; Woolcock & Narayan, 2000).

Different types of social factors such as norms and trust influence social capital in complex ways and thus make the above discussed forms more dynamic and complex at occasions.

One key aspect of the normative bias of social capital is the notion of trust. Trust is a fundamental element of social capital, as it is the glue that binds social relationships together and enables cooperation and reciprocity among individuals or groups (Coleman, 1990). Trust can be built through repeated interactions, shared values, and common interests (Putnam, 2000). However, trust can also be influenced by norms and biases that are present in a particular community or society.

Norms are the unwritten rules, expectations, and values that guide human behavior in social settings (Fukuyama, 1995). Norms can shape the formation of social capital by influencing the types of relationships that are formed, the level of trust that is established, and the opportunities that are accessed through social connections (Fukuyama, 1995). For example, in a community where there are strong norms of reciprocity and trust, bonding social capital may be highly valued, and individuals who are not part of the group may face challenges in accessing social support or opportunities (Fukuyama, 1995). This can lead to a normative bias where certain groups are favored, while others are excluded or marginalized.

Norms can also influence bridging and linking social capital. For example, in diverse communities where there are different norms, values, and interests among groups, bridging social capital may face challenges in maintaining trust and reciprocity (Putnam, 2000).

Norms can also influence the types of formal institutions that are accessed through linking social capital. For instance, in societies where there are norms of nepotism or favoritism, linking social capital may be biased toward certain individuals or groups, while others may face challenges in accessing resources or opportunities through formal institutions (Woolcock & Narayan, 2000).

Furthermore, biases, such as racial, gender, or class biases, can also impact social capital. Biases are preconceived notions or prejudices that influence our perceptions, attitudes, and behaviors toward individuals or groups based on their characteristics. Biases can affect the formation of social capital by influencing the types of relationships that are formed, the level of trust that is established, and the opportunities that are accessed through social connections. For example, biases can impact bonding social capital by reinforcing existing social hierarchies and norms that favor certain groups while excluding or marginalizing others (Putnam, 2000).

Biases can also impact bridging and linking social capital. For instance, biases can affect the level of trust and reciprocity that is established among diverse groups in bridging social capital (Putnam, 2000). Biases can also influence the types of formal institutions that are accessed through linking social capital. For example, biases can result in unequal access to resources or opportunities through formal institutions, such as government agencies or businesses, based on individuals' characteristics, such as race, gender, or class (Woolcock & Narayan, 2000).

Similarly, policies and interventions can promote linking social capital that facilitates access to formal institutions, such as government services, business networks, or educational opportunities, for individuals and groups that are marginalized or disadvantaged (Woolcock & Narayan, 2000). This can help to address existing biases and disparities in the distribution of resources and opportunities and promote greater equity and social inclusion.

Let's understand these negative sides and criticism of social capital in a more detailed fashion in the next chapter.

3

CRITIQUES OF SOCIAL CAPITAL

Here is the detailed discussion in the literature on some of the vital criticisms of social capital.

EXCLUSION AND INEQUALITY

Exclusion and inequality have emerged as significant critiques of social capital in the literature. While social capital has been lauded for its potential to foster cooperation and collaboration within communities, it has also been scrutinized for its role in perpetuating exclusion and inequality, particularly along lines of race, class, gender, and other social identities.

The critique of exclusion and inequality highlights that social capital can sometimes reinforce existing disparities rather than bridging them. Social networks and norms can be exclusive, favoring certain groups while excluding others. For example, research has shown that social capital can be influenced by racial, ethnic, and cultural homogeneity, leading to the formation of strong bonding social capital within particular communities, but creating barriers to entry for individuals from diverse backgrounds (Portes, 1998). This can result in exclusion and marginalization of certain groups from accessing resources, opportunities, and social support, perpetuating existing inequalities.

Moreover, social capital can also exacerbate class-based inequalities. Studies have shown that individuals with higher socioeconomic status tend to have greater access to social networks and resources, leading to the concentration of social capital among the privileged few (Bourdieu, 1986). This can result in a social capital gap, where individuals from marginalized and disadvantaged backgrounds have limited access to social networks and resources, putting them at a disadvantage in terms of economic, educational, and other opportunities.

Gender-based inequalities can also intersect with social capital. Research has shown that women, especially those from marginalized communities, may face gender-specific barriers in accessing social capital due to cultural norms, social expectations, and power dynamics (Kabeer, 1999). This can result in the exclusion of women from certain social networks or the undervaluing of their contributions, limiting their ability to benefit from social capital.

In addition, social capital can sometimes perpetuate exclusion and inequality through its reliance on trust and social norms. While trust is often seen as a crucial element of social capital, it can also be shaped by societal biases and discriminatory practices. Social norms within a community may not align with broader societal values or may be exclusionary in nature, leading to the exclusion of certain groups that do not conform to these norms (Fine, 2001). This can further perpetuate inequality by reinforcing existing social hierarchies and limiting the opportunities for those who do not conform to the dominant social norms.

Furthermore, the critique of exclusion and inequality also highlights the limitations of social capital in addressing structural inequalities and systemic issues. Social capital tends to focus on interpersonal relationships and networks, often neglecting the broader structural and systemic factors that shape inequality. It can sometimes divert attention away from addressing the root causes of inequality, such as discriminatory policies, unequal distribution of resources, and power imbalances, by placing emphasis solely on individual or community-level social connections.

In conclusion, while social capital has been recognized for its potential benefits, the critique of exclusion and inequality draws attention to the limitations and challenges of social capital in perpetuating disparities along the lines of race, class, gender, and other social identities. Exclusionary social networks, biased norms, and power dynamics can reinforce existing inequalities, creating barriers for marginalized groups to access social capital and its associated benefits.

INSTRUMENTALISM

Social capital has been criticized for reducing social relationships to mere resources for individual gain, leading to the exploitation and manipulation of social relationships for self-interest. Instrumentalism critiques of social capital focus on how social capital is often conceptualized and operationalized in instrumental terms, meaning that it is seen as a means to achieve specific outcomes or goals rather than as an intrinsic value in and of itself. While social capital has been lauded for its potential to facilitate cooperation, trust, and collective action, instrumentalism critiques argue that this approach can lead to a narrow and utilitarian view of social relationships, reducing them to mere tools for achieving economic or political objectives. This critique raises important questions about the ethical implications, unintended consequences, and limitations of instrumentalist approaches to social capital.

One of the main criticisms of instrumentalism is that it can lead to the commodification of social relationships. Social capital is often measured and valued based on its potential to generate economic or political outcomes, such as increased employment opportunities, access to resources, or political influence (Woolcock, 2001). This can result in the instrumental use of social relationships, where individuals and communities strategically build and leverage social networks solely for instrumental purposes rather than for genuine social interactions or community building. This instrumental approach to social capital can reduce social relationships to transactional exchanges, where the value of social ties is solely based on their utility in achieving specific objectives, leading to the instrumentalization of social interactions and undermining the authenticity and trust that underlie social capital.

Moreover, instrumentalism critiques highlight that the utilitarian focus of social capital can sometimes reinforce existing power dynamics and inequalities. Research has shown that social capital can be unequally distributed across different groups in society, with those who already have social, economic, and political advantages being better positioned to access and leverage social capital (Lin, 2000). This can perpetuate existing disparities and exacerbate inequalities, as those who are already marginalized or disadvantaged may have limited access to social capital and its associated benefits. Furthermore, instrumentalist approaches may prioritize the interests and needs of those who hold power or resources, potentially leading to the exploitation or manipulation of social relationships for personal or group gain, and further exacerbating power imbalances within communities.

In addition, instrumentalism critiques argue that the instrumental approach to social capital may prioritize short-term outcomes over long-term social well-being. The emphasis on instrumental outcomes, such as economic gains or political influence, may prioritize immediate results at the expense of broader social and community development. For example, communities or individuals may engage in transactional exchanges of social capital for short-term economic gains, such as getting a job or accessing resources, without considering the long-term social consequences or sustainability of these interactions. This can lead to a myopic focus on short-term instrumental gains, potentially neglecting the complex and multifaceted nature of social relationships and their long-term implications for community well-being and resilience.

Furthermore, instrumentalism critiques also raise concerns about the ethical implications of using social capital for instrumental purposes. Social relationships are inherently complex, multifaceted, and embedded in social, cultural, and historical contexts. Instrumental approaches to social capital may reduce these complex relationships to simplistic measures or instrumental strategies, potentially undermining the ethical considerations and social responsibilities associated with social interactions. For example, using social capital to achieve economic or political objectives without considering the ethical implications, such as the impact on vulnerable or marginalized groups, can result in unintended consequences and ethical dilemmas. This highlights the need for a more nuanced and ethical approach to understanding and utilizing social capital, recognizing the complexity and diversity of social relationships and their ethical dimensions.

Moreover, instrumentalism critiques also point to the limitations of instrumental approaches in addressing systemic issues and promoting sustainable social change. Social capital is often conceptualized as a resource that can be accumulated and utilized to achieve specific outcomes, without necessarily addressing the underlying structural factors that shape social relationships and inequalities. For example, focusing on building social networks for instrumental purposes, such as accessing economic opportunities, may not address the structural barriers that prevent certain groups from accessing social capital in the first place, such as discrimination, poverty, or social exclusion (Portes, 1998). This critique highlights that instrumental approaches to social capital may not fully capture the complex interplay between individual agency and structural factors in shaping social relationships and may overlook the need for addressing underlying systemic issues to promote sustainable social change.

Furthermore, instrumentalism critiques of social capital raise concerns about the potential for social capital to be co-opted or manipulated for political or economic agendas. Social capital has been used as a tool for political mobilization, with the assumption that strong social networks can facilitate collective action and foster civic engagement (Putnam, 2000). However, instrumentalist approaches may lead to the instrumentalization of social capital for partisan or narrow interests, where social relationships are used to advance specific political ideologies or economic agendas. This can lead to the manipulation or distortion of social capital for instrumental purposes, potentially undermining its original intent of fostering trust, cooperation, and community well-being.

Another critique of instrumentalism is that it can reinforce individualistic and neoliberal ideologies. Instrumental approaches to social capital often prioritize individual agency and strategic action, where individuals are seen as rational actors who can actively build and leverage social networks for their own benefit. This individualistic approach can align with neoliberal ideologies that emphasize personal responsibility, self-interest, and market-oriented solutions to social issues (Bourdieu, 1986). This can lead to a reductionist view of social relationships, where individuals are encouraged to engage in strategic calculations to build social capital for personal gain, without considering the broader social, cultural, and structural contexts that shape social relationships. This critique raises questions about the ideological underpinnings and potential unintended consequences of instrumental approaches to social capital.

Moreover, instrumentalism critiques also highlight the limitations of relying solely on quantitative measures to capture the complexity and diversity of social relationships. Social capital is often measured using survey-based measures, such as network size, trust, and participation in formal associations. However, these measures may not fully capture the multidimensionality and context-dependent nature of social capital. Social relationships are complex and multifaceted, and their value and meaning may vary across different cultures, communities, and contexts. Quantitative measures may overlook the qualitative aspects of social relationships, such as the quality of social ties, the nature of social interactions, and the cultural norms that shape social capital. This critique emphasizes the need for a more nuanced and contextually grounded understanding of social capital that goes beyond quantitative measures.

In addition, instrumentalism critiques raise concerns about the potential for social capital to be used as a tool for social control or exclusion. Instrumental approaches to social capital may prioritize certain types of social relationships or networks, such as those that are formal, visible, or recognized by mainstream institutions, while excluding or devaluing other types of social relationships, such as informal or marginalized networks (Lomnitz, 1977). This can result in the exclusion or devaluation of certain groups, such as minority populations, immigrants, or marginalized communities, who may have different forms of social capital that are not recognized or valued within instrumental approaches. This critique highlights the need to consider the diverse forms of social capital that exist within different communities and to avoid reinforcing existing social hierarchies or exclusionary practices.

Lastly, instrumentalism critiques raise concerns about the potential for social capital to be used as a substitute for structural interventions or policy changes. Instrumental approaches to social capital may emphasize individual or community-level interventions, such as building social networks or fostering trust, without addressing the broader structural factors that shape social relationships and inequalities (Foley & Edwards, 1999).

NORMATIVE BIAS

Social capital can be influenced by normative bias, where certain norms and values within a community may not align with the broader societal values or may be exclusionary in nature (Fine, 2001). One example of the normative bias of social capital can be seen in the formation of bonding social capital, which refers to the strong ties and close relationships within homogenous groups, such as family, close friends, or members of the same cultural or ethnic community.

Portes (1998) found that bonding social capital among immigrants can reinforce ethnic boundaries and limit opportunities for social integration into the wider society. This normative bias can perpetuate social inequality by excluding individuals who do not share the same norms or do not belong to the dominant group. Bonding social capital can provide social support and facilitate collective action within the group, but it can also lead to exclusion and marginalization of individuals who do not belong to the group. For instance, in a study of social capital in immigrant communities, another example of the normative bias of social capital can be observed in the formation of bridging social capital, which refers to the weak ties and connections between different groups or communities. Bridging social capital can facilitate information flow, social mobility, and access to resources through diverse networks (Granovetter, 1973). However, bridging social capital is not equally accessible to all individuals and communities. For instance, studies have shown that individuals from marginalized or disadvantaged backgrounds, such as racial and ethnic minorities, may face barriers in accessing bridging social capital due to discrimination, bias, or cultural differences (Klinenberg, 2018; Lin, 2001). This normative bias can contribute to the perpetuation of social inequalities by limiting opportunities for individuals from marginalized groups to access resources and opportunities through diverse networks. Furthermore, the normative bias of social capital can also be observed in the formation of linking social capital, which refers to the connections and networks between individuals or communities and formal institutions, such as government, organizations, or institutions (Woolcock, 1998). Linking social capital can facilitate collective action, advocacy, and engagement with formal institutions for social change (Woolcock, 1998). However, the access to linking social capital can be influenced by factors such as social class, education, or political power, which can create disparities in the ability to engage with formal institutions (Jessop et al., 2013). For example, studies have shown that individuals with higher levels of education and socioeconomic status are more likely to have access to linking social capital and participate in formal institutions, while those from lower socioeconomic backgrounds may face barriers.

LACK OF AGENCY AND POWER DYNAMICS

Social capital can be seen as constraining individual agency, as individuals may feel pressured to conform to social norms and networks rather than pursue their own interests or goals (Woolcock, 2001).

At the same time, power dynamics influences social capital, where certain individuals or groups may have more access to social networks and resources, leading to the concentration of social capital among the privileged few (Kabeer, 1999). And for this reason, social capital may not have universal applicability, as its effects may be contingent upon specific cultural, social, and economic contexts, limiting its generalizability (Foley & Edwards, 1999).

Social capital can have inherent contradictions, as social networks and norms may simultaneously foster cooperation and trust but also lead to exclusion and discrimination (Sampson, 1999).

ETHICAL CONCERNS

Social capital can raise ethical concerns, as individuals may feel pressured to engage in social relationships solely for instrumental gain, leading to ethical dilemmas and exploitation (Fine, 2001). One ethical concern of social capital is its potential to exacerbate inequalities and exclusions. Social capital is often built through social networks, and those who have access to influential networks may have advantages over others. However, not everyone has equal access to social networks, and this can perpetuate existing inequalities. For example, people from marginalized or low-income backgrounds, minority groups, or marginalized communities may face barriers in accessing social networks, resulting in limited social capital and reduced opportunities for economic and social advancement (Putnam, 2000). This raises ethical concerns about fairness and social justice, as social capital may concentrate power and resources in the hands of a few, exacerbating existing disparities. Another ethical concern is the potential for social capital to be used for unethical purposes, such as corruption, cronyism, and nepotism. Social capital can be used to consolidate power and exclude outsiders, leading to favoritism and unfair treatment (Portes, 1998). This can undermine trust and fairness in institutions and perpetuate inequality and injustice. For instance, research has shown that in societies with high levels of social capital, there may be increased opportunities for corruption as social connections can be leveraged for personal gain, resulting in unethical behavior (Uslaner, 2005). This raises ethical concerns about integrity, transparency, and accountability in the utilization of social capital. Furthermore, social capital can be context-dependent, and its effects may not always be positive. Social capital that is based on exclusive or homogeneous networks can lead to social polarization and reinforce existing divisions within a society (Woolcock, 2001). In some cases, social capital can be used to promote harmful practices, such as discrimination, racism, or other forms of prejudice, if the social networks that are being relied upon for social capital are based on shared discriminatory beliefs or practices (Portes, 1998). This raises ethical concerns about inclusivity, diversity, and social cohesion, as social capital may inadvertently perpetuate discriminatory attitudes or practices. Measuring social capital can also pose ethical challenges. Unlike financial capital or physical assets, social capital is intangible and can be challenging to measure accurately. This can limit the effectiveness of social capital as a policy tool, as it may be difficult to assess and evaluate the impact of interventions aimed at promoting social capital (Foley & Edwards, 1997). Additionally, there is a lack of consensus on how social capital should be defined and operationalized, which can further complicate efforts to study and understand its effects (Bourdieu, 1986). This raises ethical concerns about validity, reliability, and accountability in the measurement and use of social capital data, as flawed measurements or misinterpretations can have unintended consequences. Another ethical concern is that social capital may not always lead to meaningful social change or address structural issues. While social capital can facilitate cooperation and collective action, it may not always be effective in addressing systemic problems, such as poverty, inequality, or discrimination. Structural issues often require broader changes in policies, institutions, and power dynamics rather than just relying on individual or group-level social connections (Fine, 2001). This raises ethical concerns about effectiveness, sustainability, and impact, as social capital interventions may fall short in addressing deep-rooted societal challenges.

MEASUREMENT CHALLENGES

Measuring social capital can be challenging, as it is a multifaceted and context-dependent concept, and different measures may yield varying results, leading to issues of validity and reliability (Carpiano, 2006).

One of the primary measurement concerns of social capital is the conceptualization and definition of the construct. Social capital has been defined and conceptualized in various ways by different scholars and researchers, leading to inconsistency in its measurement. Some define social capital in terms of structural features, such as social networks and the resources embedded in them, while others emphasize cognitive and normative aspects, such as trust, norms, and values (Coleman, 1988; Putnam, 2000). This lack of a universally accepted definition and conceptual framework for social capital can result in measurement approaches that capture different aspects of social capital or even contradict each other, leading to confusion and inconsistency in research findings (Szreter & Woolcock, 2004).

Validity, or the accuracy of measurement, is another concern in the measurement of social capital. Validity refers to the extent to which a measurement accurately captures the intended construct. Social capital is a complex and multifaceted construct, and it can be challenging to accurately measure all its dimensions. For instance, measuring trust or norms, which are crucial components of social capital, may require subjective self-report measures, and individuals' responses may be influenced by social desirability bias or cultural factors, leading to potential measurement errors (Woolcock, 1998). Moreover, social capital can be context-dependent, meaning that its meaning and significance can vary across different cultural, social, and geographical contexts, further complicating the measurement process and raising concerns about the generalizability of findings (Szreter & Woolcock, 2004).

Reliability, or the consistency of measurement, is another important concern in the measurement of social capital. Reliability refers to the extent to which a measurement produces consistent results when applied repeatedly to the same sample or population. Social capital measures should be reliable to ensure that the same results are obtained when measuring the same construct multiple times. However, measuring social capital can be challenging due to its dynamic and evolving nature, as social networks, norms, and trust can change over time. Moreover, different measurement methods or instruments may yield different results, further complicating the issue of reliability in social capital measurement (Bourdieu, 1986).

Context-dependence is another concern in the measurement of social capital. Social capital can be influenced by various contextual factors, such as culture, geography, and historical context. Different contextual factors can shape the nature and significance of social capital in a particular context, making it difficult to compare social capital across different contexts. For example, the meaning and impact of social networks or norms may vary significantly across different cultural or geographical settings, leading to potential measurement biases and challenges in interpreting findings (Woolcock, 1998).

Interpretation of social capital measurements is another concern. Social capital measures can be complex and multifaceted, and interpreting findings can be challenging due to the lack of a clear framework or guidelines. Researchers may face difficulties in interpreting the meaning and implications of social capital measures, particularly when different measures are used or when the findings are inconsistent. Moreover, the potential for misinterpretation or misrepresentation of social capital measures can lead to inaccurate or misleading conclusions, further complicating the interpretation process (Szreter & Woolcock, 2004).

Addressing these measurement concerns of social capital is crucial to ensure the accuracy, reliability, and validity of research findings. Several strategies can be employed to mitigate these concerns and improve the measurement of social capital. Firstly, researchers need to clearly define and conceptualize social capital based on a solid theoretical framework to ensure consistency and comparability across studies. This requires a thorough review of existing literature and an explicit definition of social capital that encompasses all relevant dimensions.

Secondly, researchers should use multiple measures or methods to capture different dimensions of social capital. For example, a combination of self-report measures and objective measures, such as network analysis or observation, can provide a more comprehensive assessment of social capital. This can help mitigate the issue of measurement error and provide a more accurate and reliable assessment of social capital.

Thirdly, researchers should consider the context-dependence of social capital and tailor their measurement approaches accordingly. This includes accounting for cultural, geographical, and historical context in the measurement process and interpreting findings in light of these contextual factors. This can help ensure the validity and generalizability of research findings across different contexts.

Furthermore, researchers should also consider the issue of reliability in social capital measurement. Longitudinal studies that measure social capital over time can help assess its stability and changes, and the use of standardized measurement instruments can enhance the consistency and reliability of measurements.

Lastly, researchers should be cautious in interpreting social capital measurements and should strive for a nuanced and contextually sensitive interpretation. This includes being aware of the limitations and potential biases of different measurement approaches, considering alternative explanations for findings, and avoiding overgeneralization or misrepresentation of results (Szreter & Woolcock, 2004).

Measurement concerns are significant challenges in the assessment of social capital. The multidimensional and intangible nature of social capital, along with its context-dependent and evolving characteristics, make its measurement complex and challenging. Addressing these concerns through clear conceptualization, validity, reliability, context-dependence, and nuanced interpretation is crucial for accurate and meaningful assessment of social capital. Researchers should carefully consider these concerns and employ appropriate strategies to enhance the measurement of social capital, thereby contributing to a more robust and reliable understanding of its role and impact in various domains of society.

MIXING THE SOCIAL CAPITAL WITH OTHER CONCEPTS

As policymakers and researchers continue to explore the concept of social capital, it is important to be aware of these critiques and consider the limitations and complexities associated with its fundamental concept that kept producing the application ambiguity and criticism. For instance, is social norm really a form of social capital? It seems Coleman and many following scholars missed the idea that social capital may or may not generate new norms and is also affected by the social norms itself. For instance, the social capital formed by a student group playing basketball may decide to follow (not follow) a social norm of other student group playing hockey or soccer.

The dynamics of trust within the context of social capital are intriguing and multifaceted. Trust plays a pivotal role in various social interactions, whether between individuals, communities, or institutions. When we consider the relationship between an individual and their government, it is tempting to assume that trust necessitates frequent interactions and the gradual building of a relationship. However, trust is a complex phenomenon that can manifest differently in various contexts, and it is not always contingent on direct, ongoing engagement. To better comprehend the intricate interplay between trust and social capital, we must also examine the analogous phenomenon of trust in brands and explore how these dynamics relate to broader social organizations and policies. This analysis will shed light on the nuanced nature of trust, its role in building and utilizing social capital, and the limitations of traditional scholarly approaches in capturing these complexities.

The concept of trust is multifaceted and takes on various forms and degrees of intensity. When we consider trust in the context of the relationship between an individual and their government, it is common to envision a process where trust is gradually built through repeated interactions. Traditionally, this notion holds that trust is the product of positive experiences, transparency, and reliability on the part of the government. In such a scenario, trust acts as an indicator of social capital, suggesting that individuals have established a favorable network or relationship with their government, characterized by mutual respect and cooperation.

However, this traditional understanding of trust does not encapsulate the full breadth of its manifestations. Trust can, in fact, take on different forms and emerge in unexpected ways. Consider the relationship between consumers and brands. In the consumer world, individuals often place their trust in brands without engaging in frequent or direct interactions with the company that produces those brands. We regularly purchase products or use services offered by these brands, and our trust in them is based on a variety of factors, including their reputation, track record, and the quality of their offerings. In essence, our trust in these brands is a form of social capital, a resource that we can leverage for our benefit, such as making informed choices or enjoying reliable products.

This phenomenon challenges the notion that trust always follows a linear progression of interaction and relationship-building. While trust in government might indeed evolve through ongoing interactions, trust in brands illustrates that it can also be established through indirect, transactional interactions. This deviation from the conventional understanding of trust prompts us to reconsider how social capital is built and utilized in various contexts.

Moreover, trust in broader social organizations, including government and other institutions, can often be influenced by the policies and benefits they provide rather than direct personal relationships. Individuals may trust their government not necessarily because they have interacted frequently with government officials but because they perceive tangible benefits from government policies, such as social services, infrastructure, or economic stability. In such cases, trust is a reflection of the utility of the institution rather than a measure of social capital in the traditional sense.

This brings us to an important question: does trust always equate to social capital? While trust can certainly be an element of social capital, it is not the sole determinant. Social capital encompasses a broader spectrum of social networks, norms, and relationships. It includes not only trust but also the resources and support that individuals can access through their connections. Thus, while trust is an integral part of social capital, it is only one facet of a more comprehensive mechanism.

Furthermore, scholars have often struggled to capture the full complexity of social capital, including the role of trust, in their research methodologies. Traditional approaches may overlook the subtle nuances of trust and its manifestations in different contexts. This limitation in scholarly analysis can hinder our understanding of how trust operates within social capital networks and how it impacts individuals and communities.

To delve deeper into this complexity, it is crucial to explore the role of place attachment in the context of social capital. Place attachment refers to the emotional connection individuals have to a specific geographic location, such as a neighborhood, town, or region. This attachment can influence trust and social capital dynamics. For example, people who feel a strong attachment to their place of residence may be more inclined to trust local institutions, including the government, as they perceive these institutions as integral to the well-being of their community.

However, place attachment is not a one-size-fits-all concept, and its relationship with social capital is intricate. People may also develop place attachment to locations they wish to leave due to negative experiences or dissatisfaction. In such cases, place attachment may not necessarily translate into trust or social capital. This underscores the importance of considering individual experiences and sentiments when examining the link between place attachment, trust, and social capital.

In essence, trust within the context of social capital is a multifaceted phenomenon that defies a one-dimensional understanding. It can emerge through diverse pathways, including direct interactions, transactional relationships, and the perception of benefits from institutions. While trust is undoubtedly a component of social capital, it should not be conflated with the entirety of social capital's complex dynamics.

CRITIQUES OF DIGITAL SOCIAL CAPITAL

Despite its potential benefits, digital social capital has been subject to criticism and contestation. One of the key critiques of digital social capital is the issue of social inequality and exclusion. Research has shown that not all individuals have equal access to digital social capital, as it is shaped by factors such as race, gender, socioeconomic status, and geographic location (Hargittai, 2010). This digital divide can exacerbate existing social inequalities, creating disparities in individuals' ability to access and benefit from digital social capital (DiMaggio et al., 2004).

Another critique of digital social capital is the issue of online surveillance, privacy, and data exploitation. Social media platforms and other online platforms often collect and use individuals' data for targeted advertising, content curation, and algorithmic decision-making, raising concerns about the commodification of social capital and the erosion of privacy (boyd & Crawford, 2012). Additionally, the spread of fake news, misinformation, and online harassment can also undermine the trust and authenticity of digital social capital, posing challenges to its viability and effectiveness (Pennycook et al., 2018).

SUMMARY OF THE CRITIQUES

Social capital can contribute to the reproduction of existing social hierarchies, where certain groups have more access to resources, opportunities, and social support, while others face challenges in accessing these benefits (Putnam, 2000; Woolcock & Narayan, 2000). This can perpetuate social inequalities and exacerbate existing disparities among different groups in society (Putnam, 2000; Woolcock & Narayan, 2000). For example, in communities where bonding social capital is predominantly formed within homogenous groups, it can result in exclusion of individuals or groups who do not belong to the dominant group, leading to social segregation and marginalization.

Similarly, biases in social capital can reinforce existing inequalities and perpetuate discrimination. Biases based on race, gender, class, or other characteristics can result in unequal access to social capital, where certain groups are favored, while others face barriers in forming social connections, accessing resources, or opportunities (Woolcock & Narayan, 2000). This can result in a further stratification of society, where certain groups have more social capital and advantages, while others are disadvantaged and face limited opportunities for social, economic, and political participation (Woolcock & Narayan, 2000).

The normative bias of social capital can also have implications for policy and interventions aimed at promoting social cohesion, community development, and social well-being. Many policies and interventions rely on social capital as a means to achieve positive outcomes, such as increased civic engagement, improved health outcomes, or economic development (Kawachi et al., 1997). However, if social capital is biased and unevenly distributed, these policies and interventions may inadvertently reinforce existing social hierarchies, norms, and biases and perpetuate inequalities (Kawachi et al., 1997; Woolcock & Narayan, 2000).

For example, policies that aim to strengthen bonding social capital within homogenous communities may reinforce exclusionary practices and perpetuate social segregation rather than promoting inclusivity and diversity (Putnam, 2000). Similarly, policies that rely on bridging and linking social capital may not be effective if there are existing biases or norms that limit the level of trust and reciprocity among diverse groups (Putnam, 2000). Biases in social capital can also result in unequal access to formal institutions, such as government services or business opportunities, leading to further disparities (Woolcock & Narayan, 2000).

In order to address the normative bias of social capital, it is important to acknowledge and understand the social, cultural, and historical context in which social capital operates. Social capital is shaped by a complex interplay of factors, including social norms, values, biases, historical legacies, and power dynamics (Fukuyama, 1995; Putnam, 2000). Therefore, interventions and policies aimed at promoting social capital should take into account these contextual factors and strive to address the underlying biases and inequalities that influence the formation, distribution, and utilization of social capital (Woolcock & Narayan, 2000).

One approach to addressing the normative bias of social capital is to promote inclusive and diverse forms of social capital. For example, policies and interventions can promote bridging social capital that promotes interactions and relationships among diverse groups and facilitates the development of trust and reciprocity among individuals with different backgrounds, identities, and interests. Bridging social capital can help to break down social barriers, reduce prejudice and biases, and promote social cohesion in diverse communities.

One of the main criticisms of social capital is that it can be exclusionary and exacerbate inequalities. Social capital is often built through social networks, such as friendships, family ties, and professional associations. However, not everyone has equal access to these networks. Those who are marginalized or excluded from certain social groups or networks may have limited access to social capital, which can perpetuate existing inequalities. For example, people from low-income backgrounds, minority groups, or marginalized communities may face barriers in accessing social networks, resulting in limited social capital and reduced opportunities for economic and social advancement.

Another critique of social capital is that it can be used for nefarious purposes. While social capital is often seen as a positive force that promotes trust and cooperation, it can also be used for negative purposes, such as corruption, cronyism, and nepotism. In some cases, social capital can be used to consolidate power and exclude outsiders, leading to favoritism and unfair treatment. This can undermine social cohesion and trust in institutions and perpetuate inequality and injustice.

Furthermore, social capital can be context-dependent and may not always result in positive outcomes. For example, social capital that is based on exclusive or homogeneous networks can lead to social polarization and reinforce existing divisions within a society. In some cases, social capital can be used to promote harmful practices, such as discrimination, racism, or other forms of prejudice, if the social networks that are being relied upon for social capital are based on shared discriminatory beliefs or practices.

Critics of social capital also argue that it can be difficult to measure and quantify. Unlike financial capital or physical assets, social capital is intangible and can be challenging to measure accurately. This can limit the effectiveness of social capital as a policy tool, as it may be difficult to assess and evaluate the impact of interventions aimed at promoting social capital. Additionally, there is a lack of consensus on how social capital should be defined and operationalized, which can further complicate efforts to study and understand its effects.

Another criticism is that social capital can have limitations in promoting social change and addressing structural issues. While social capital can facilitate cooperation and collective action, it may not always be effective in addressing systemic problems, such as poverty, inequality, or discrimination. Structural issues often require broader changes in policies, institutions, and power dynamics rather than just relying on individual or group-level social connections.

Social capital is largely criticized for the dangers of its outcome that is largely influenced by various factors, e.g., it is blamed to be exclusionary, context-dependent, difficult to measure, etc. Besides these long existing problems, the serious trouble caused is due to the fundamental confusion of the term with other vital concepts such as trust, norms, and attachment.

4

IMPLICATIONS OF SOCIAL CAPITAL

Before we get lost into the ever evolving buzz word of social capital, we must get back to the basics of the term to understand its origin, ambiguity, and contestation and then try to understand its implications. Social capital has significant policy implications as it can influence various aspects of society, including community development, economic growth, health outcomes, and social cohesion. Social capital can enhance social cohesion by building trust, empathy, and understanding among diverse groups in society. Policies that promote social capital, such as intergroup dialog programs, community-building initiatives, and policies that reduce social disparities, can foster social cohesion, reduce social conflicts, and promote inclusivity and social harmony.

Social capital can facilitate the implementation of public policies by fostering networks, trust, and cooperation among different stakeholders, including government, civil society, and communities. Policies that promote social capital, such as participatory decision-making processes, collaborative governance, and community engagement initiatives, can improve the effectiveness and sustainability of public policy implementation. Following are some practical applications for policymakers and practitioners of social capital.

COMMUNITY DEVELOPMENT

Social capital can foster trust, cooperation, and civic engagement within communities, leading to increased community development. Policies that promote social capital can encourage community participation, volunteering, and collaboration, which can contribute to the development of social networks and mutual support systems within communities.

Community development and social capital are intertwined concepts that play a crucial role in fostering stronger and more resilient communities. Community development refers to the process of enhancing the well-being of a community by addressing its economic, social, and environmental needs and promoting active participation and engagement among community members (Fawcett et al., 1995). Social capital, on the other hand, refers to the networks, relationships, norms, and trust that exist within a community, which facilitate cooperation, collaboration, and mutual support among community members (Putnam, 1995). Together, community development and social capital can create a foundation for community resilience, economic growth, and social cohesion.

Box 1

· ·

Community-Driven Development (CDD) Programs.

The World Bank has implemented Community-Driven Development (CDD) programs in developing countries that aim to empower local communities by leveraging social capital. CDD programs involve participatory decision-making processes, community mobilization, and community-led initiatives to address local development challenges. These programs rely on social networks, community organizations, and local knowledge to identify and implement development projects that are relevant and beneficial to the community (Word Bank, 2017).

Community development involves a range of activities and approaches aimed at improving the quality of life in a community. These activities can include community organizing, capacity building, community-based initiatives, and participatory decision-making processes (Gittell & Vidal, 1998). Community development seeks to empower community members, build their skills and capacities, and foster a sense of ownership and responsibility toward their community. Social capital is a critical element of community development as it helps to facilitate the interactions and relationships among community members, which are necessary for effective community development efforts.

Social capital encompasses various forms, including bonding, bridging, and linking social capital (Woolcock & Narayan, 2000). Bonding social capital refers to the close relationships and strong ties that exist among individuals within a particular group, such as family, friends, or members of a religious or cultural community. Bridging social capital, on the other hand, refers to the relationships and connections that exist across different groups or communities, fostering connections and collaborations among diverse individuals or groups. Linking social capital involves the relationships and networks that individuals or communities have with institutions and organizations, such as government agencies, nongovernmental organizations, or other formal entities.

The concept of social capital has gained significant attention in community development literature and practice due to its positive impacts on community well-being. Social capital has been found to contribute to various outcomes, including increased civic engagement, improved health and well-being, enhanced economic development, and stronger social cohesion (Putnam, 2000; Woolcock, 1998). Social capital can foster trust, cooperation, and reciprocity among community members, leading to increased collaboration, collective action, and community resilience (Pretty & Ward, 2001). In this section, we will explore the ways in which social capital can contribute to community development.

CIVIC ENGAGEMENT AND PARTICIPATION

Social capital can facilitate civic engagement and participation in community development efforts. Trust and networks among community members can lead to increased participation in community activities, such as volunteering, community organizing, and local decision-making processes (Cunningham, 2002). Social capital can also promote collective action, where community members come together to address common challenges and work toward common goals (Woolcock, 2001). Through civic engagement and participation, community members can contribute their knowledge, skills, and resources to address community needs, build community assets, and promote social change (Fawcett et al., 1995).

Research has shown that communities with higher levels of social capital tend to have higher levels of civic engagement and participation (Putnam, 2000). For example, a study by Verba et al. (1995) found that communities with higher levels of social capital, as measured by indicators such as civic associations, trust, and political participation, tended to have higher voter turnout rates and greater levels of political engagement. Similarly, a study by Cunningham (2002) found that communities with higher levels of social capital, as measured by indicators such as community involvement, trust, and social networks, were more likely to have active community organizations and higher levels of community participation in decision-making processes.

Box 2

. . . .

Asian Development Bank Interventions.

Asian Development Bank improved water and sanitation while strengthening local governance through 34 projects in Nepal and other south Asian countries (Carroll, 2001). In the above case, a detailed discussion on conceptualization and practice of social capital is linked with the policy intervention that improved the quality of life and political empowerment. The case resembles with the empowering local governance that has widely been claimed throughout multiple interventions by donor agencies.

ECONOMIC DEVELOPMENT AND ENTREPRENEURSHIP

Social capital can also play a significant role in promoting economic development and entrepreneurship in communities. Networks and relationships among community members can create opportunities for economic exchange, collaboration, and innovation (Putnam, 2000). Social capital can foster trust and cooperation among local businesses, encourage knowledge sharing and learning, and facilitate access to resources, information, and markets (Coleman, 1988). Additionally, social capital can create social norms and expectations that promote ethical business practices and discourage opportunistic behavior, thus creating a favorable environment for entrepreneurship and economic growth (Burt, 1997).

Research has shown that communities with higher levels of social capital tend to have more vibrant local economies and higher levels of entrepreneurship (Flora & Flora, 1993). For example, a study by Grootaert and Van Bastelaer (2002) found that social capital, as measured by indicators such as trust, social networks, and civic engagement, was positively associated with entrepreneurship in communities in developing countries. Another study by Knack and Keefer (1997) found that communities with higher levels of social capital, as measured by indicators such as trust and membership in civic associations, had higher levels of economic growth and investment.

SOCIAL COHESION AND INCLUSION

Social capital can also contribute to social cohesion and inclusion within communities. Social networks and relationships can foster a sense of belonging and identity among community members, create a shared sense of purpose, and promote mutual understanding and respect (Putnam, 2000). Social capital can also facilitate the inclusion of marginalized or vulnerable groups, such as immigrants, minorities, or low-income individuals, by providing access to resources, information, and support networks (Chaskin, 1997).

Box 3

Social Protection Programs by World Bank.

The World Bank has used social capital in the design and implementation of social protection programs in developing countries. Social protection programs, such as cash transfer programs or social insurance schemes, often require strong social networks and community support for effective targeting, delivery, and utilization of benefits. Social capital can facilitate the identification of vulnerable populations, enhance the targeting accuracy of social protection programs, and promote community cohesion and mutual support (Grootaert, 2010).

Furthermore, social capital can help reduce social conflicts and promote social harmony by facilitating communication, cooperation, and negotiation among community members (Woolcock & Narayan, 2000).

Research has shown that communities with higher levels of social capital tend to have greater social cohesion and inclusion (Pretty & Ward, 2001). For example, a study by Halpern (2005) found that communities with higher levels of social capital, as measured by indicators such as trust, social networks, and civic engagement, tended to have lower levels of crime and violence, higher levels of social trust, and more cohesive social relationships. Another study by DeFilippis (2001) found that social capital, as measured by indicators such as civic associations and networks, played a critical role in promoting social inclusion and empowerment in low-income communities in the United States.

Policymakers and practitioners can leverage social capital to build stronger and more resilient communities by incorporating social capital considerations into their community development strategies.

Policies that promote civic engagement and participation can help build social capital in communities. This can be done through supporting local community organizations, creating opportunities for community members to participate in decision-making processes, and fostering a culture of active citizenship. Community-based initiatives, participatory planning processes, and collaborative governance approaches can help promote civic engagement and participation, leading to increased social capital and community empowerment.

ECONOMIC DEVELOPMENT

Social capital can positively impact economic growth by facilitating business networks, information sharing, and entrepreneurial activities. Policies that promote social capital, such as networking events, business mentoring programs, and access to social networks, can foster economic development, innovation, and entrepreneurship. Policies that foster economic development and entrepreneurship can also promote social capital in communities. This can be done through providing access to resources, information, and networks for local businesses, promoting knowledge sharing and innovation, and supporting entrepreneurship training and mentoring programs. Policies that create a favorable environment for business collaboration, networking, and cooperation can contribute to the development of social capital, leading to economic prosperity.

Box 4

. . . .

Rural Development Interventions.

Rural communities often rely on social networks and social norms for agricultural production, natural resource management, and marketing. The World Bank has supported rural development programs that foster social capital, such as farmer cooperatives, community-based resource management, and collective marketing initiatives, to enhance rural livelihoods and sustainable rural development (Dasgupta & Serageldin, 2000).

Within economic dimension, microfinance is one of the most significant success policies that uses the concept of social capital. The World Bank has used social capital in microfinance programs in developing countries. Microfinance programs provide financial services, such as microloans and savings, to low-income individuals and communities. Social capital, such as trust and social networks, plays a critical role in microfinance programs as it enables group-based lending approaches, peer monitoring, and social collateral that can enhance repayment rates and financial inclusion. The World Bank has supported microfinance programs that leverage social capital, such as village savings and loan associations (VSLAs) and self-help groups (SHGs), to promote financial access and poverty reduction (Fox & Gershman, 2000).

HEALTH OUTCOMES

Social capital can impact health outcomes through its influence on access to health care, health behaviors, and social support. Social capital and community health policy are two interconnected concepts that recognize the significance of social relationships, networks, and community engagement in promoting positive health outcomes. Social capital refers to the resources, trust, and social connections that exist within a community, while community health policy encompasses the strategies and interventions aimed at improving the health and well-being of individuals within a community.

Research has consistently shown that social capital plays a crucial role in enhancing community health outcomes. Strong social networks and social support systems have been associated with reduced morbidity and mortality rates, improved mental health, and better health behaviors. For instance, a study by Kawachi and Berkman (2001) found that individuals with high levels of social capital had lower rates of depression, higher levels of self-rated health, and reduced all-cause mortality. Similarly, House et al. (1988) demonstrated that individuals with greater social ties experienced better health outcomes, including lower rates of cardiovascular disease.

Community health policies often prioritize the development and maintenance of social capital as a means of improving health outcomes. These policies may include initiatives that encourage community participation, volunteerism, and social cohesion. For example, community garden programs have been implemented in various communities, aiming to promote social connections and improve health. A study by Litt et al. (2015) found that individuals involved in community gardens reported higher social cohesion, increased physical activity, and improved overall well-being.

Furthermore, community health policies may focus on building community-based organizations and partnerships to address health disparities and promote equitable access to health care. These policies recognize that social networks and trust between residents and health care providers are essential for effective health care utilization. Butterfoss et al. (1993) highlighted the significance of community coalitions in improving health outcomes through collaborative efforts and community engagement.

In addition, community health policies may aim to enhance social capital by creating supportive environments that facilitate health-promoting behaviors. For instance, policies promoting walkable neighborhoods, accessible parks, and safe public spaces encourage social interaction and physical activity, fostering social capital and improved community health. Cohen et al. (2000) emphasized the role of structural factors in shaping health behaviors and highlighted the importance of policy interventions that create favorable conditions for health.

To effectively implement community health policies that enhance social capital, collaboration between multiple stakeholders is crucial. Local government agencies, community-based organizations, health care providers, and residents need to work together to identify community needs, design interventions, and ensure their sustainability. Such collaborative efforts can foster community empowerment, ownership, and social cohesion, ultimately leading to improved health outcomes.

Scheffler et al.'s (2008) study focuses on the relationship between social capital and health outcomes in developing countries. The author reviews existing literature and empirical evidence to explore how social capital, defined as the social networks, relationships, norms, and trust within communities, can impact health outcomes in developing countries.

The author argues that social capital can have both direct and indirect effects on health outcomes. Direct effects include social support networks that provide emotional support, information sharing, and resources for better health management. Indirect effects include the influence of social networks on health behaviors, health care utilization, and community engagement in health-related activities.

Box 5

. . . .

Community Health Worker Programs.

CHW programs, which involve trained community members providing health services within their communities, have been widely used in many developing countries as a health policy intervention. CHW programs leverage social capital by utilizing the existing social networks and relationships within communities to promote health behaviors, provide health education, and facilitate access to health care services. CHWs, who are often recruited from the local community, can build trust and rapport with community members, which can enhance the acceptability and effectiveness of health interventions. By leveraging social capital, CHW programs can improve health outcomes, particularly in underserved communities (UNICEF, 2020).

Scheffler and Brown highlight that social capital can be a valuable resource for improving health outcomes in resource-constrained settings. They discuss how community-based health programs, such as community health worker (CHW) programs, can leverage social capital to promote health behaviors and enhance access to health care services.

Policies that promote social capital, such as community-based health programs, social support programs, and policies that reduce social inequalities, can contribute to better health outcomes for individuals and communities. Policy interventions that leverage social capital can have significant implications for health outcomes.

Box 6

. . . .

India's Self Help Groups in COVID Period.

India's SHGs have produced over 19 million masks during COVID in 2020 (World Bank, 2020). The press information bureau (PIB) of India released the highlighting the achievement of flagship scheme in India. The mask making has brought smiles to the faces of many women across the country. Their testimony is visible on the PIB release. The SHGs made under the livelihood mission acted as a rescuer in the difficult COVID times by generating masks at the same time generating livelihood for group members.

Social support networks, such as support groups or peer-led interventions, leverage social capital by creating platforms for individuals with chronic diseases to connect, share experiences, and provide mutual support. These networks can help individuals manage their chronic conditions by providing emotional support, sharing information and resources, and promoting healthy behaviors. Social support networks have been used in health policy interventions for chronic diseases such as HIV/AIDS, diabetes, and cancer to improve disease management, adherence to treatment, and overall quality of life.

In conclusion, social capital and community health policy are intertwined concepts that recognize the importance of social relationships, networks, and community engagement in promoting positive health outcomes. Research has consistently shown that social capital is associated with improved health outcomes, while community health policies often aim to build and strengthen social capital as a means of improving community health. By fostering social connections, promoting community engagement, and creating supportive environments, these policies can enhance social capital and contribute to better overall health in communities.

RESILIENCE AND DISASTER RECOVERY

Social capital can contribute to resilience and disaster recovery efforts by strengthening community bonds, mutual support systems, and information sharing networks. Policies that promote social capital, such as disaster preparedness programs, community resilience initiatives, and social networks for disaster recovery, can enhance the ability of communities to cope with and recover from disasters. Disaster Risk Management Programs: The World Bank has recognized the importance of social capital in disaster risk management programs in developing countries. Strong social networks, community organizations, and trust among community members can enhance disaster preparedness, response, and recovery.

The World Bank and United Nations have supported disaster risk management programs that leverage social capital, such as community-based early warning systems, local disaster management committees, and participatory disaster risk assessments, to enhance resilience and reduce vulnerability to disasters (Sanyal & Routray, 2016).

Box 7

· ·

Disaster Risk Resilience.

There is another example of disaster risk resilience from my own experience in Bihar, India, in 2010 where a German donor organization funded community group projects in flood-affected area of Sitamarhi district of Bihar (India) by making groups of men and women and that of children for food grain banking, awareness of their rights, and that for their education.

I was in charge of 10 villages, and the project was ongoing before I joined the civil society organization in Bihar. By making groups and repeated interactions between the community members, they probably felt more supported, but I cannot say whether they got any political empowerment or any significant improvement in their lives as an outcome of social capital because I could not see impact evaluation report of the program intervention. The entire project team including me never used the term "social capital", for us, groups were formed for internal lending and borrowing of medicines, and food grains.

If we are to apply the concept of social capital in the above example, I would probably now think that the groups were holding social capital, and the outcome was the support that group members got in difficult times. All the factors such as the norms (men and women had separate groups), physical barriers (remote geographical location on river side), and social factors (caste, age, and education level) were the influencers in making the groups. Let us compare these groups with the group of children aimed to educated them about disasters and prepare them to face the flood. Was there any outcome of social capital out of children groups? Certainly, in nonfinancial forms. For example, improved learnings, lending and borrowing of books, and other study materials. Though, we cannot certainly say how much was the improvement in their resilience due to lack of any impact evaluation report during my tenure. Can we take these groups as a proxy to social capital? If yes, in what sense? It is clear that groups of adults had financial or economic nature of gains, whereas group of children had nonfinancial gains that might have improved their cognitive ability and coping capacity against disasters. Let us take this case beyond the villages; federations of farmers (kisaan sangathan) and that of women (mahila sangathan) were made by combining the respective community village groups and that of children groups. The women and children could raise their voices through these aggregated federations. The aggregated social capital in terms of federations gives an opportunity to demand for the members' rights. However, there is always a threat of political use of these federations because these community-based federations lack constitutional power to exercise their rights they are demanding for. Now, with the increasing age of digital technology, the groups and federations have more reach and efficient communication system through digital connectivity (mobiles and internet). In the coming subsections, we will see how digitalization of social capital can lead to positive outcomes and reducing the barriers to achieve those positive outcomes of social capital.

APPLICATIONS OF DIGITAL SOCIAL CAPITAL

Digital social capital, despite facing certain criticisms and challenges, has found application in various domains, contributing to positive outcomes in the realms of public health, disaster response, education, and entrepreneurship and innovation. This concept represents the value embedded in online social networks, communities, and relationships, and its utilization is evident in several areas where it plays a significant role in fostering collaboration, sharing knowledge, and providing support.

In the field of public health, digital social capital has been harnessed to promote health-related behaviors, such as smoking cessation, regular exercise, and healthy eating. Research by Valente et al. (2015) highlights the use of online support groups, social networks, and health apps in this context. These digital platforms serve as spaces where individuals facing similar health challenges can connect, share experiences, and offer encouragement. By leveraging digital social capital, public health initiatives can tap into the collective wisdom and motivation of these communities, ultimately leading to improved health outcomes.

Disaster response and crisis management have also seen the positive impact of digital social capital. Online networks and communities provide valuable resources during times of crises. Liu et al. (2018) underscore the importance of digital social capital in disaster response efforts. Through these online channels, individuals can rapidly disseminate critical information, coordinate relief efforts, and offer emotional support to those affected. The digital realm facilitates the formation of ad hoc crisis response communities, allowing for efficient and timely assistance.

In the realm of education, digital social capital has been applied to enhance learning and knowledge sharing. Online communities of practice, collaborative platforms, and peer-to-peer networks have become hubs for educational interaction and information exchange. Kimmons et al. (2017) emphasize the role of digital social capital in promoting learning. These platforms enable educators and learners to connect across geographical boundaries, exchange insights, and access a diverse range of educational resources. The collective knowledge and expertise within these digital networks contribute to enriched learning experiences.

Entrepreneurship and innovation benefit significantly from the application of digital social capital. Hargadon and Sutton (1997) emphasize the role of social networks and online communities in facilitating knowledge sharing, mentorship, and access to resources among entrepreneurs and innovators. Digital platforms enable individuals with entrepreneurial aspirations to connect with mentors, investors, and fellow innovators. These connections provide valuable guidance, financial support, and collaborative opportunities, fostering innovation and the growth of start-ups.

In conclusion, digital social capital has demonstrated its potential for positive outcomes across various domains. In public health, it facilitates health behavior promotion by connecting individuals in online support groups and health-focused communities. In disaster response, it plays a crucial role in providing information, resources, and emotional support during crises. In education, it enhances learning and knowledge sharing through online communities of practice and collaborative platforms. In entrepreneurship and innovation, it fosters collaboration, mentorship, and resource access among aspiring entrepreneurs and innovators. These applications underscore the value of digital social capital in harnessing the collective power of online networks and communities to address diverse societal challenges and opportunities.

CRITICAL ANALYSIS OF THE LESSONS LEARNED FROM THE INTERVENTIONS

Policies that promote social capital can contribute to community development, economic growth, health outcomes, social cohesion, effective public policy implementation, and resilience to challenges and disasters. It is important for policymakers to consider the role of social capital in their policy decisions and strategies for promoting societal well-being.

After all these cases and ideas discussed about using the social capital, we see largely, development interventions are based on community groups, and it seems groups are considered as a social capital base of all the community intervention programs. For example, the largest community group intervention of SHGs in India.

It seems from the above cases that interventions using the social capital notion rely on making groups to leverage the social capital generated through their networks. The question is – whether people implementing the interventions were aware of social capital in all the cases? For example, the concept of SHGs emerged out of social capital? Perhaps not. Mad. Younus experiment of successful lending in Bangladesh has germinated the idea of microfinance practices that can be done successfully with women and that by forming their groups (Yale University, 2011). We see the emergence of literature that largely has "imposed" the idea of economic benefit of social capital to capture the success of initial microfinance interventions. Whether the two (social capital and microfinance practice) developed in isolation and later merged together by scholars and policy makers, they fit well together. At present, no one denies the form of social capital that exists in the community groups. But what remains unaddressed is the refined understanding of the social capital and its implication on policy implications of the term.

Let's get back to the origin again, who forms a group? To get an answer to this, if we understand deeply, people with similar socioeconomic backgrounds tend to come together. Network scientists term it homophily, and classic sociologists may term it traditional solidarity. Once individuals come together, they try to solve their problem (income improvement, better education, better water and sanitation facility, better governance). So, the togetherness of the individuals is process of formation of social capital that is only realized inform of improved income, health facility access, and trust in government. The mistake scholars often make is to take these outcomes as a proxy to social capital. And often term some social relations (e.g., emotional support or sexual relations) as a (bonding) social capital that may not necessarily be made or used cautiously to use as a capital. What is the alternative then? It is a hard ask; what can be said at this point is unless we know individuals make "conscious" relations to form a group to achieve an outcome, we cannot term the relation as social capital. It may be emotional support (crying on shoulder, sympathy) or sexual relation or walking together to enjoy the weather or to improve health. Certainly, people do not necessarily come together all the time with inherent beneficial motive to generate a form of capital. Many a time, in scholarly pursuits of terming a social phenomenon, relations are put under the umbrella of social capital. These confusions arise largely due to changing frame of reference. At a microlevel, we do not usually make relations all the time for a benefit or using the relations as a capital. However, at the macrolevel, we make groups and associations to protect our rights, solve a problem, or to get more bargaining power, i.e., coming together to reach an improved situation.

At the microlevel, individuals do not always form relationships with the explicit goal of generating social capital. In everyday life, people interact with others for a myriad of reasons, including socializing, emotional support, or personal enjoyment, without necessarily viewing these interactions as a means to accumulate social capital. These interpersonal relationships are often based on trust, reciprocity, and shared experiences, and they form the foundation of social networks.

Conversely, at the macrolevel, we observe the formation of groups and associations that serve as conduits for generating and leveraging social capital. These groups are typically organized around common interests, shared goals, or collective identities. Their primary purpose is often to protect individual or collective rights, solve complex problems, or enhance bargaining power. In this context, individuals come together to pool their social resources, knowledge, and influence to achieve outcomes that would be difficult or impossible to attain individually.

From a policy perspective, it becomes evident that external interventions can play a pivotal role in catalyzing the formation of such groups. Communities may require incentives or triggers to organize themselves effectively and align their efforts with development goals. For instance, microfinance groups can be incentivized through financial support to promote economic development in impoverished areas. Similarly, health groups can be formed to improve access to health care services, with interventions such as training and resource provision acting as catalysts for their establishment.

From a community's standpoint, the reasons for grouping together can vary widely. One common motivation is to address shared challenges through collective actions or social movements. These challenges may encompass issues related to social justice, environmental sustainability, or economic disparities. Communities recognize the strength in numbers and the potential to effect change when they pool their social capital. Social movements, for instance, often emerge as a response to perceived injustices, where individuals and groups unite to advocate for systemic reforms.

Therefore, the concept of social capital can be perceived differently depending on the level of analysis and perspective taken. At the microlevel, individuals engage in social interactions for various personal reasons, not necessarily with the explicit intent of accumulating social capital. However, at the macrolevel, groups and associations are formed to leverage social capital for collective benefits, and external interventions can play a role in facilitating these processes. Ultimately, the dynamics of social capital are shaped by a complex interplay of individual motivations, community needs, and policy interventions, all of which contribute to the broader understanding of how social networks and relationships influence societal outcomes.

Nonetheless, from the policy standpoint, we can say that there is always an attempt to form a group, and groups are usually formed when individuals get incentive in the designed interventions. For instance, microfinance groups for economic benefits, health groups for improved health access, and so on. So, from an external interventionist's point of view, a community always needs a trigger or stimulus to make groups that align with the goals of development interventions. From a community's standpoint, they group together to solve a problem, e.g., collective actions or social movements.

5

CONCLUSION AND FUTURE DIRECTIONS

The foremost conclusion that we must draw that the implications of social capital in the modern times go beyond academia, as they have practical implications for various stakeholders, including policymakers, organizations, practitioners, scholars, and individuals.

After all these concepts and cases, can we put social capital in a single frame for an easier understanding? Let's take a pause and break the word "social capital" into two separate meaning full words: "social" and "capital". It seems we have come a long way without much consideration on the term "capital" that largely has three meanings: a place (city), a resource for business (benefit purpose), or punishment for severe crime in law. Certainly, throughout the chapters, we have been concerned about benefit (financial or nonfinancial) both in social relations. Given this capital augmented idea of *social capital*, we cannot certainly take every relation as a proxy for social capital. Rather, we often begin with relations that may or may not turn out to be a social capital that is only recognizable based on its outcome (financial, emotional, job attainment, or other nonfinancial support). The scholarships right from the beginning have failed to take this outcome-oriented comprehensive view of social capital. In other words, once we use social relations for any benefit, then only the connection becomes social capital; otherwise, it is just a relation or just a group of same class, same village or colony, or same town. Likewise, trust in government or big associations may not necessarily reflect my social capital, rather it is the outcome that may be of my neighbors.

Fig. 6 shows our idea of social capital so far in a simplistic manner.

Social capital is often conceptualized in different stages, i.e., as a starting point (mostly individual centric relations), informal groups (friends, community clubs), formal groups (legal associations, formal relations at work place).

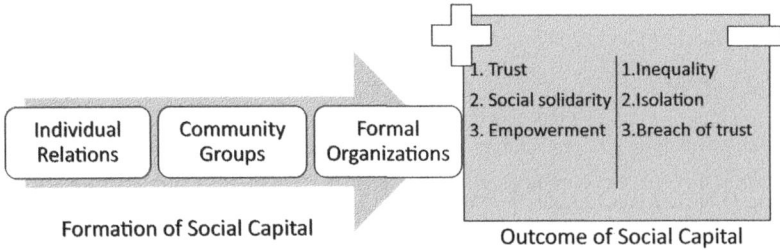

	1. Trust	1.Inequality
Individual Relations	Community Groups	Formal Organizations
2. Social solidarity	2.Isolation
3. Empowerment	3.Breach of trust

Formation of Social Capital   Outcome of Social Capital

Fig. 6. Simplistic Summary of Social Capital.

To understand the term social capital, let us assume an individual who relates with individual's surroundings, e.g., human (need based relations), place (emotional attachment to a place based on birth, employment, education etc.), and other man-made social entities (associations, groups, family). When the relations of human take a form where the humans get any benefit (economic: job or money access), emotional (close family and friends in relation), education, or any kind of support they would have never gained as an individual, they reach to a situation where they can access a pool of resources created through the aggregation of the relational entities and access those as and when needed.

In accessing the social capital, one may face barriers, and likewise, the outcome of social capital may vary. So, many of the assumptions about social capital are fundamentally wrong in the sense that outcome of social capital is treated as proxy to social capital, e.g., trust, empowerment, solidarity in society. Since inception stages, even the factors affecting the formation of social capital are misunderstood as social capital. For example, social norms influence the way individuals interact with each other and hence accelerate or decelerate the formation of groups (social capital). Likewise, power in different forms produces the ill-effects in terms of making a social group to work in the favor of powerful group members (e.g., elite capture). Isolation of individuals, breach of trust, and inequality are some of the side effects produced by the misuse of power over social capital. So, we must be careful in distinguishing the influencing factors and outcomes of social capital.

Here are the key takeaways for the conceptual understanding of social capital and its potential implications for practice.

WHAT DID WE UNDERSTAND ABOUT SOCIAL CAPITAL?

We can infer from the varying meanings of social capital that the social relations build basic premise of social capital.

Social capital is *aggregated entity* that arises from connected social actors to benefit the connected member(s). Without measuring outcome arising out of the social relation, we can never term the relation(s) as social capital. To understand better, bifurcate the terms into social and capital, and then, we will get a sense that the term is a form of capital that comes out of social entity, i.e., relations between social actors those range from individual to social organizations. Community-based organizations (self-groups in developing countries, community support groups in the west), large associations (national associations of lawyers), clubs (youth and other formalized groups for entertainment), and formalized form of governments (elected democratic institutions) all are the result of social capital and often used in studies as a proxy to measure the concept. In its primitive form, it originates between individuals through relations. The individual need to connect to the surrounding (friends, family, partners, and colleagues) develops a premise of networked relations that forms a basic foundation of mutual support and trust. Once people start getting benefit out of these relations – financial help, emotional support, medical assistance without paying for the same – these relations work as a social capital. So, trust is an outcome of social relations that has the potential to become a social capital.

Though not all the members in a social relation can get benefits at the same time, no relation can be treated as capital unless individual(s) in the relation get some benefit (monetary or nonmonetary). It is also possible that a few may get benefits at the expense of loss of other members of the groups. For example, in more formalized social groups, key position holders may get favorable benefit of the formalized group than the other members, e.g., presidents, secretaries, and ministers of powerful social groups (lawyers, police, and state governments). Thus, in order to understand social capital, we should conceptualize the connections as a social entity (friends, family, organizations, and governments) and assess whether those more or less formalized connections are useful to individual(s) connected in the entity. In big formalized social organizations, e.g., large associations, not all the individuals get benefits all the time. Hence, the possibility of unequal distribution of social capital benefits always exists due to inherent inequality of society. The various factors that act as a force of inclusion–exclusion (e.g., race and gender) and segregation in the society also affect the aggregated social connections (social capital). Although once developed in a group, the social capital may act as an enabler to enforce pre-existing social norms or improved trust between group members; yet, it can never be a norm or trust itself. So treating the norms and trust as a proxy to social capital is a wrong way to assess the same. Additionally, norms may themselves create/hinder the formation of relations between people and hence affect the realization of social capital benefits.

HOW CAN POLICYMAKERS AND ORGANIZATIONS USE THE IMPROVED UNDERSTANDING OF SOCIAL CAPITAL?

The foremost thing is to avoid earlier ambiguity of social capital concept and confuse the essence of the traditional terms of norms, trust, and emotions (sense of belongingness) with the proxy measures of social capital. One must remember that the social entities only become *social capital* when combined with the economic connotation of capital which has the primary motif of benefit – the benefits that individuals seek in various forms, e.g., emotional support, attainment of job, attainment of improved income, access to institutions and so on. Policymakers and external agencies must think – When social is just social and when it becomes or has a potential to become a capital? Not all the time, people invest in relations to accrue a monetary benefit, and this noneconomic nature of building relations is the essence of social capital that keeps it separate from the other forms of capital.

Bourdieu cautioned about elite capture on social capital long ago. The elites are not uniform category of all the society, and given the individualistic and community-based interventions in many cases of social capital application, one must avoid such capture right from the social capital building stages. The intervening agencies should take a caution that all the social entities are shaped by the social factors that are not favorable to everyone in the society, and hence, interventionists must build guard for those who can potentially be excluded when social becomes capital due to their intervention. Also, many a times, intervening agencies should design the program in a way that outcomes of social capital may not be hijacked by a few or distributed unequally among the groups.

Policy interventions through education policies look forward to convert the humans into human capital; organizational intervention to build community groups for economic and social empowerment of community members uses the aggregated relations (social capital) of members to get better health, economic, and sometimes political outcomes.

Thus, policymakers can leverage social capital in the digital era to inform policy decisions, promote social cohesion, and engage citizens in civic and political activities. We have discussed ample real-life examples and cases where social capital is applied to yield encouraging results for the community welfare. In the digital era, a comprehensive realization of the digitization of social capital is yet to be realized. There are anecdotal cases that we discussed in the implication chapter, and there could be numerous ways in which policymakers can use social capital insights in the digitized world. For example, governments can design educational policies that leverage online networks for learning and skill development, create strategies to combat misinformation and polarization in online political discourse, and facilitate inclusive and diverse online communities. Policymakers can also develop guidelines and regulations to promote responsible and ethical use of social capital in the digital era, such as protecting individuals' privacy, data security, and digital rights.

Organizations can leverage social capital in the digital era to promote collaboration, innovation, and employee engagement. For example, organizations can create online platforms or communities to foster knowledge sharing, collaboration, and networking among employees, customers, and other stakeholders. Organizations can also incorporate social capital measures in their performance evaluation and reward systems, recognizing the value of social connections and networks for organizational success. Businesses can also leverage social capital to enhance customer relationships, brand loyalty, and market presence. For instance, companies can utilize social media platforms to build and engage with online communities of customers, influencers, and brand advocates, fostering social capital that can positively impact their bottom line.

Educators can leverage social capital in the digital era to enhance learning experiences and promote digital literacy among students. For example, educators can use online networks and social media platforms to facilitate collaborative learning, connect students with experts and mentors, and promote peer-to-peer knowledge sharing. Educators can also teach students critical digital literacy skills, such as evaluating the credibility of online information, understanding the implications of social capital in online networks, and promoting responsible online behaviors.

HOW DOES IT MATTER FOR INDIVIDUALS?

Individuals can leverage social capital in the digital era to enhance their social networks, access information and resources, and promote their personal and professional development. For example, individuals can actively engage in online communities and networks related to their interests, hobbies, or professional fields, building (online) social capital that can provide them with access to valuable information, opportunities, and support. Individuals can also use social media platforms to build and maintain relationships with others, fostering social capital that can enhance their well-being, career prospects, and social connectedness.

Thus, social capital in the digital age provides individuals with a wide range of opportunities to connect, collaborate, and leverage their online social networks for various purposes. From networking and knowledge sharing to crowdfunding and social activism, individuals can use social capital to enhance their personal and professional lives, access new resources, and create positive social change. However, it is important to be mindful of ethical considerations, such as privacy, information accuracy, and digital literacy, when utilizing social capital in the digital era. By leveraging social capital effectively and responsibly, individuals can harness the power of online social networks for their benefit and contribute to the growth and development of digital communities. In these cautions of ethical and responsible use, individuals should building their own defense mechanism in getting exploited (dating apps), monetary fraud (scams for job, selling products etc.). The risks in modern times has gone many fold, but the digital revolution has also given the plenty of opportunity to safeguard and maintain transparency in formation and usage of social capital for the benefit of individuals and that for the aggregate groups and society.

HOW HAS DIGITALIZATION INFLUENCED THE SOCIAL CAPITAL?

One of the most prominent effects of digitalization is the unprecedented level of connectivity it has facilitated. Digital technologies, especially the internet and social media platforms, have transcended geographical barriers and enabled individuals to connect with others globally. This interconnectedness has led to the formation of diverse networks that transcend physical boundaries, allowing people to communicate and collaborate with individuals from different cultures, backgrounds, and perspectives.

This increased connectivity has broadened social networks and enabled the sharing of ideas, experiences, and knowledge on an unprecedented scale. Social media has played a crucial role in amplifying marginalized voices and shedding light on social injustices. Movements like the Arab Spring and the Black Lives Matter movement have leveraged digital platforms to mobilize people and raise awareness about critical issues. This ability to mobilize and organize digitally has transformed the dynamics of collective action and advocacy.

While acknowledging these positive impacts, it's important to remain mindful of the challenges and potential negative consequences that can arise from the rapid integration of digital technologies into our lives.

One of the most visible negative effects is reduction in physical interaction. The making of social capital shifts away from physical to virtual mode. Most important is the spatial dimension; if the virtual connectivity helps in accelerating the social capital formation that goes beyond the geographical territory, it is likely to benefit individuals seeking to benefit from their immediate geographical location. For example, someone from a remote village aspiring to take a job in foreign countries would benefit the most with connections outside his local territory. Likewise, influencing the international government organizations would require such virtual social capital that spans beyond locations of individuals' local place. However, the same may not work true when people need a trustworthy relationship with local government or municipality or escorting to take to hospital for that matter. So, the digitalization has added a complexity in social capital formation that is virtual, and it may or may not help generating an effective outcome. However, it definitely reduces the risk of misuse of social capital when regulated effectively. For example, social media groups regulating the group member's expression. At the same time, digitalization may add to the inequality where people may have access to improved devices and features that people with poor accessibility cannot access. A differentiated access to social media platforms (e.g., ordinary, prime membership) is a live example.

FUTURE WORK

Future research should focus on understanding the nuanced and evolving nature of social capital in the digital era, examining the impact of emerging technologies on social capital, investigating the dark side of social capital, exploring the intersectionality of social capital, and investigating its role in shaping organizational and societal outcomes. These areas of research can provide valuable insights for policymakers, organizations, educators, and individuals to leverage social capital for positive outcomes in the digital era.

Social capital in the digital era is a complex and dynamic phenomenon that has significant implications for individuals, organizations, societies, and policymakers. It has the potential to promote positive outcomes, such as social cohesion, trust, innovation, and collective action. However, it also has the potential for negative consequences, such as misinformation, polarization, and exclusion. As we continue to navigate the rapidly changing digital landscape, it is crucial to further our understanding of social capital dynamics in online networks and explore future directions and implications.

To conclude, we can say that social capital in the modern period is a multifaceted and dynamic phenomenon with wide-ranging implications. It has the potential to shape the way we interact, communicate, and collaborate in online networks and has significant implications for individuals, organizations, and societies as a whole. Understanding the future directions and implications of social capital in the digital era is crucial for policymakers, organizations, educators, and individuals to navigate the digital landscape effectively and promote positive outcomes for individuals and communities. Further research, guided by interdisciplinary and multi-method approaches, can contribute to our understanding of social capital in the digital era and inform evidence-based policies, practices, and interventions to harness the potential of social capital for the betterment of society.

APPENDIX: DIGITAL CAPITAL BIBLIOMETRIC REVIEW

I begin with the most basic question on concept of digital capital by offering a systematic review of the digital capital concept that gives us an idea of the past 22 years of research on the topic. After a careful in-depth review of the popular and recent literature, I reconfigure the temporally scattered ideas of digital capital visible in the literature so far.

Fig. 7 shows the methodology process that can be understood in two major steps.

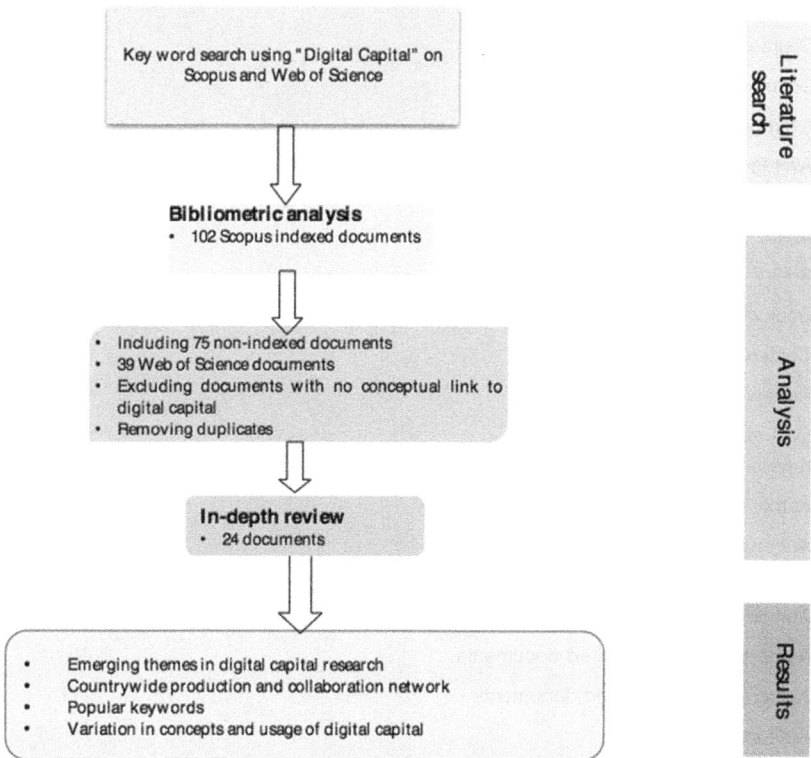

Key word search using "Digital Capital" on Scopus and Web of Science

Bibliometric analysis
- 102 Scopus indexed documents

- Including 75 non-indexed documents
- 39 Web of Science documents
- Excluding documents with no conceptual link to digital capital
- Removing duplicates

In-depth review
- 24 documents

- Emerging themes in digital capital research
- Countrywide production and collaboration network
- Popular keywords
- Variation in concepts and usage of digital capital

Literature search

Analysis

Results

Fig. 7.   Methodology Process.

I used Scopus database to search "Digital Capital" key word that yielded 102 indexed documents and 75 non-indexed documents, exporting the database in bibtex and csv format. Since the research is new and evolving, to make it more inclusive, I also included web of science database (39) that were incorporated for the in-depth review after removing the duplicate documents. I used the bibtex format to run bibliometric analysis using the "bibliometrix" package in Rstudio (Aria & Cuccurullo, 2017; Derviş, 2020). The package gives a comprehensive result on thematic trends, country production, collaboration, and keyword networks. Table 5 gives the summary of the documents used in the analysis.

Table 5. Summary of the Digital Capital Related Documents Used in Analysis.

Main Information About Data	
Timespan	1993:2022
Sources (Journals, Books, etc.)	91
Documents	102
Average years from publication	4.44
Average citations per documents	8.853
Document Types	
Article	77
Book	2
Book chapter	6
Conference paper	15
Review	2
Document Contents	
Keywords plus (ID)	359
Author's keywords (DE)	390
Authors	
Authors	207
Author appearances	229
Authors of single-authored documents	30
Authors of multiauthored documents	177
Authors Collaboration	
Single-authored documents	33
Authors per document	2.03
Co-authors per documents	2.25
Collaboration index	2.57

The bibliometric analysis was further supplemented by in-depth review of the abstracts of the top cited literature. After including 75 non-indexed documents, I removed the repeated documents and the documents having no publication trace (no doi, title, and abstract). I selected only those papers for the in-depth review that have the word "digital capital" in their title or abstract. Finally, I retained the 24 publications that contributed to the conceptual understanding of digital capital.

Further the same was supplemented by using the keyword on Google scholar database to corroborate the findings with some top cited publications.

The upcoming result section discusses the two types of results coming out of the analysis in detail.

THEMATIC MAPPING AND EVOLUTION

Cobo et al. (2011) discuss identifying, analyzing, and visualizing method of thematic evolution in a research field and Courtial (1994) suggests a coward analysis of identifying the emerging terms in the research field. The bibliometric package operationalizes these ideas to reveal some informative features about the research (Fig. 8).

Themes in the upper right quadrant are both well-developed and important for the structuring of a research field. They are known as the motor themes of the specialty, given that they present strong centrality and high density. The placement of themes in this quadrant implies that they are related externally to

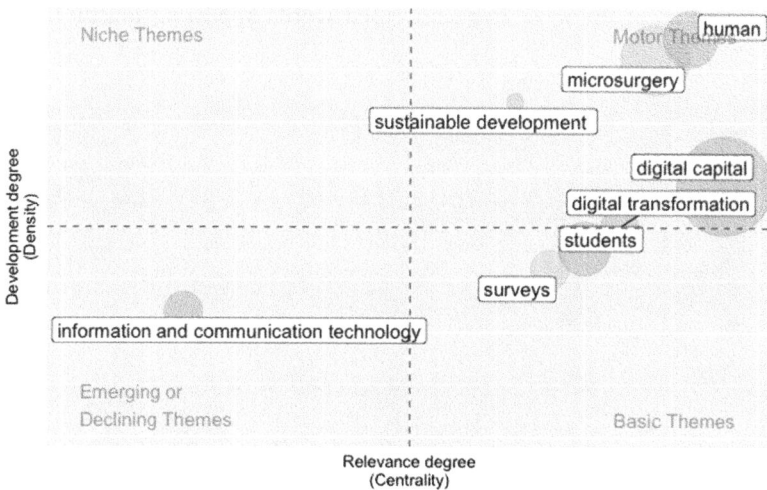

Fig. 8.   Thematic Mapping of Digital Capital Research.

concepts applicable to other themes that are conceptually closely related. Themes in the upper left quadrant have well-developed internal ties but unimportant external ties and so are of only marginal importance for the field. These themes are very specialized and peripheral in character. Themes in the lower left quadrant are both weakly developed and marginal. The themes of this quadrant have low density and low centrality, mainly representing either emerging or disappearing themes. Themes in the lower right quadrant are important for a research field but are not developed. So, this quadrant groups transversal and general, basic themes.

Digital capital and digital transformation are dominant themes followed by sustainable development and human-oriented research in the motor theme quadrant. Appearance of "microsurgery" term indicates relevance of the digital capital research for health sector. Education is another important sector that often links with information and communication technology (ICT) in the form of digital learning, e-learning as "students" word come up as one of the basic themes.

The theme ICT is an age-old term and its rate of growth in the academia is probably declining or constant that's why it is placed in the third quadrant of declining theme. It is still important and integral part of digital activities and research.

The Sankey diagram of thematic evolution (Fig. 9) suggests digital capital emerged along with internet in the past decade and gained popularity in the recent past five years or so.

The keyword network (Fig. 10) also proves that content analysis followed by analytic hierarchy process, and website was popular in the early stages of knowledge building. For keyword networks, I used Louvain criteria to cluster the networks of the most frequently used words appearing together in the

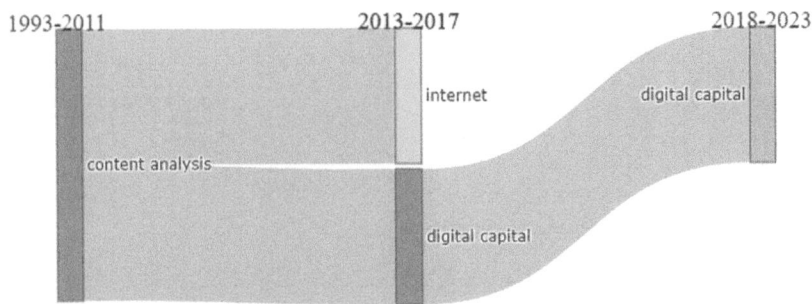

Fig. 9.   Thematic Evolution in Digital Capital Research.

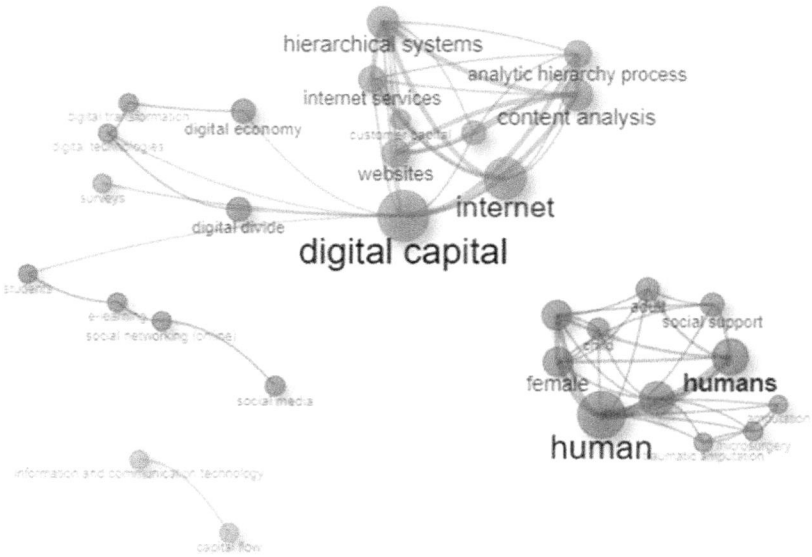

Fig. 10.   Co-Occurrence of Keywords in Digital Capital Research.

research. The emerging human(s) term indicates human-centric application of digital capital research. There are a few niche areas e.g., students and e-learning, and digital economy that indicates its importance in the education and business world.

REFERENCES

Aria, M., & Cuccurullo, C. (2017). Bibliometrix: An R-tool for comprehensive science mapping analysis. *Journal of Informetrics*, *11*(4), 959–975. https://doi.org/10.1016/j.joi.2017.08.007

Bannykh, G. (2020). *Digital capital and the labor market: Factors of mutual influence*. https://doi.org/10.2991/aebmr.k.200312.420

Bannykh, G., & Kostina, S. (2022). Measuring digital capital: Methodological approaches. *KnE Social Sciences*, 96–103. https://doi.org/10.18502/kss.v7i2.10282

Bimber, B. (1999). The Internet and citizen communication with government: Does the medium matter? *Political Communication*, *16*(4), 409–428. https://doi.org/10.1080/105846099198569

Bimber, B., Flanagin, A. J., & Stohl, C. (2012). Reconceptualizing collective action in the contemporary media environment. *Communication Theory*, *22*(4), 311–326.

Bimber, B., & Jorba, L. (2010). The impact of digital media on citizenship in a global perspective. In *Comparing digital politics* (pp. 21–70).

Blau, P. M. (1964). *Exchange and power in social life*. Wiley.

Bourdieu, P. (1986). The forms of capital. In J. Richardson (Ed.), *Handbook of theory and research for the sociology of education* (pp. 241–258). Greenwood Publishing Group.

Boyd, d., & Crawford, K. (2012). Critical questions for big data: Provocations for a cultural, technological, and scholarly phenomenon. *Information, Communication & Society*, *15*(5), 662–679.

Boyd, D., & Ellison, N. (2008). Social network sites: Definition, history, and scholarship. *Journal of Computer-Mediated Communication*, *13*, 210–230.

Brehm, J., & Rahn, W. (1997). Individual-level evidence for the causes and consequences of social capital. *American Journal of Political Science, 41*(3), 999–1023.

Brulle, R. J., & Pellow, D. N. (2006). Environmental justice: Human health and environmental inequalities. *Annual Review of Public Health, 27,* 103–124.

Bubnov, V., Kopilevich, V., & Istomina, A. (2021). Evolution of digital capital in organizations: A quantitative assessment. *Journal of Telecommunications and the Digital Economy, 9*(4), 1–22. https://doi.org/10.18080/jtde.v9n4.435

Bughin, J., & Manyika, J. (2013). *Measuring the full impact of digital capital.*

Burt, R. S. (1992). *Structural holes: The social structure of competition.* Harvard University Press.

Burt, R. S. (1997). The contingent value of social capital. *Administrative Science Quarterly, 42*(2), 339–365.

Burt, R. (2005). *Brokerage and closure: An introduction to social capital.* Oxford University Press.

Butterfoss, F. D., Goodman, R. M., & Wandersman, A. (1993). Community coalitions for prevention and health promotion. *Health Education Research, 8*(3), 315–330.

Calderón Gómez, D. (2021). The third digital divide and Bourdieu: Bidirectional conversion of economic, cultural, and social capital to (and from) digital capital among young people in Madrid. *New Media & Society, 23*(9), 2534–2553. https://doi.org/10.1177/1461444820933252

Carpiano, R. M. (2006). Toward a neighborhood resource-based theory of social capital for health: Can Bourdieu and sociology help? *Social Science & Medicine, 62*(1), 165–175. https://doi.org/10.1016/j.socscimed.2005.05.020

Carroll, T. F. (2001). *Social capital, local capacity building, and poverty reduction* (ISBN: 9715613411). Asian Development Bank.

Chaskin, R. J. (1997). Perspectives on neighborhood and community: A review of the literature. *Social Service Review, 71*(4), 521–547.

Cobo, M. J., López-Herrera, A. G., Herrera-Viedma, E., & Herrera, F. (2011). An approach for detecting, quantifying, and visualizing the evolution of a research field: A practical application to the Fuzzy sets theory field. *Journal of Informetrics, 5*(1), 146–166. https://doi.org/10.1016/j.joi.2010.10.002

Cohen, D. A., Scribner, R. A., & Farley, T. A. (2000). A structural model of health behavior: A pragmatic approach to explain and influence health behaviors at the population level. *Preventive Medicine*, *30*(2), 146–154.

Coleman, J. S. (1988). Social capital in the creation of human capital. *American Journal of Sociology*, *94*(Supplement), S95–S120.

Coleman, J. S. (1990). *Foundations of social theory*. Harvard University Press.

Cook, K. S., & Emerson, R. M. (1978). Power, equity and commitment in exchange networks. *American Sociological Review*, *43*(5), 721–739.

Cook Lin, N., & Burt, R. S. K. (2001). *Social capital: Theory and research*. Aldine de Gruyter.

Courtial, J. P. (1994). A coword analysis of scientometrics. *Scientometrics*, *31*(3), 251–260. https://doi.org/10.1007/BF02016875

Cunningham, I. (2002). Developing human and social capital in organisations. *Industrial & Commercial Training*, *34*(3), 89–94. https://doi.org/10.1108/00197850210424926

Darcy, S., Yerbury, H., & Maxwell, H. (2019). Disability citizenship and digital capital: The case of engagement with a social enterprise telco. *Information, Communication & Society*, *22*(4), 538–553. https://doi.org/10.1080/1369118X.2018.1548632

Dasgupta, P., & Serageldin, I. (2000). *Social capital A multifaceted perspective*. The International Bank for Reconstruction and Development/The World Bank.

DeFilippis, J. (2001). The myth of social capital in community development. *Housing Policy Debate*, *12*(4), 781–806. https://doi.org/10.1080/10511482.2001.9521429

Derviş, H. (2020). Bibliometric analysis using bibliometrix an R package. *Journal of Scientometric Research*, *8*(3), 156–160. https://doi.org/10.5530/jscires.8.3.32

DiMaggio, P., Hargittai, E., Celeste, C., & Shafer, S. (2004). From unequal access to differentiated use: A literature review and agenda for research on digital inequality. *Social Inequality*, 355–400.

Dudwick, N., Kuehnast, K., Jones, V. N., & Woolcock, M. (2006). Analyzing social capital in context: A guide to using qualitative methods and data. In *The international bank of reconstruction and development*. The World Bank. https://doi.org/10.1016/j.jml.2007.09.002

Ellison, N. B., Steinfield, C., & Lampe, C. (2007). The benefits of Facebook "friends": Social capital and college students' use of online social network sites. *Journal of Computer-Mediated Communication, 12*(4), 1143–1168.

Ellison, N. B., Gray, R., Lampe, C., & Fiore, A. T. (2014). Social capital and resource requests on Facebook. *New Media & Society, 16*(7), 1104–1121. https://doi.org/10.1177/1461444814543998

Ellison, N. B., Vitak, J., Gray, R., & Lampe, C. (2014). Cultivating social resources on social network sites: Facebook relationship maintenance behaviors and their role in social capital processes. *Journal of Computer-Mediated Communication, 19*(4), 855–870.

Fawcett, S. B., Paine-Andrews, A. L., Francisco, V. T., Schultz, J. A., Richter, K. P., Lewis, R. K., Williams, E. L., Harris, K. J., Berkley, J. Y., Fisher, J. L., & Lopez, C. M. (1995). Using empowerment theory in collaborative partnerships for community health and development. *American Journal of Community Psychology, 23*, 677–697.

Field, J. (2003). *Social capital.* Taylor & Francis Group Publication.

Fine, B. (2001). *Social capital versus social theory: Political economy and social science at the turn of the millennium.* Routledge.

Flap, H., & Völker, B. (2001). Goal specific social capital and job satisfaction effects of different types of networks on instrumental and social aspects of work. *Social Networks, 23*, 297.

Flora, C. B., & Flora, J. L. (1993). Entrepreneurial social infrastructure: A necessary ingredient. *The Annals of the American Academy of Political and Social Science, 529*, 48–58. http://www.jstor.org/stable/1048623

Foley, M. W., & Edwards, B. (1997). Escape from politics? Social theory and the social capital debate. *American Behavioral Scientist, 40*(5), 550.

Foley, M. W., & Edwards, B. (1999). Is it time to disinvest in social capital? *Journal of Public Policy, 19*(2), 141–173.

Fox, J., & Gershman, J. (2000). The world bank and social capital: Lessons from ten rural development projects in the Philippines and Mexico. *Policy Sciences, 33*(3/4), 399–419. http://www.jstor.org/stable/4532512

Fukuyama, F. (1995). *Trust: The social virtues and the creation of prosperity.* Free Press.

Fukuyama, F. (2001). Social capital, civil society and development. *Third World Quarterly, 22*(1), 7–20. http://www.jstor.org/stable/3993342

Gil de Zúñiga, H. (2012). Social media use for news and individuals' social capital, civic engagement and political participation. *Journal of Computer-Mediated Communication, 17*(3), 319–336. https://doi.org/10. 1111/j.1083-6101.2012.01574.x

Gittell, R., & Vidal, A. (1998). *Community organizing: Building social capital as a development strategy*. Sage Publications.

Granovetter, M. (1973). The strength of weak ties. *American Journal of Sociology, 78*(6), 1360–1380.

Grootaert, C. (2010). *Social capital: The missing link (English)*. Social Capital Initiative working paper series; no. 3. World Bank Group. http://documents. worldbank.org/curated/en/902971468764409654/Social-capital-the-missing-link

Grootaert, C., & van Bastelaer, T. (2002). *Understanding and measuring social capital: A synthesis of findings and recommendations from the social capital initiative*. World Bank.

Grusky, D., & Lin, N. (2019). Social networks and status attainment. *The Inequality Reader, 25*(May), 594–596. https://doi.org/10.4324/ 9780429494468-62

Halpern, D. (2005). *Social capital*. Polity Press.

Hanifan, L. J. (1916). The rural school community center. *Annals of the American Academy of Political and Social Science, 67*, 130–138.

Hargadon, A. B., & Sutton, R. I. (1997). Technology brokering and innovation in a product development firm. *Administrative Science Quarterly*, 716–749.

Hargittai, E. (2010). Digital na(t)ives? Variation in internet skills and uses among members of the "net generation". *Sociological Inquiry, 80*(1), 92–113.

House, J. S., Landis, K. R., & Umberson, D. (1988). Social relationships and health. *Science, 241*(4865), 540–545.

Ignatow, G., & Robinson, L. (2017). Pierre Bourdieu: Theorizing the digital. *Information, Communication & Society, 20*(7), 950–966. https://doi.org/10. 1080/1369118X.2017.1301519

Jessop, B., Moulaert, F., Hulgard, L., & Hamdouch, A. (2013). Social innovation research: A new stage in innovation analysis. In F. Moulaert (Ed.), *The international handbook on social innovation: Collective action, social learning and transdisciplinary research* (pp. 110–130). Edward Elgar.

Kabeer, N. (1999). Resources, agency, achievements: Reflections on the measurement of women's empowerment. *Development and Change, 30*(3), 435–464.

Kawachi, I., & Berkman, L. F. (2001). Social ties and mental health. *Journal of Urban Health, 78*(3), 458–467.

Kawachi, I., Kennedy, B. P., Lochner, K., & Prothrow-Stith, D. (1997, September). Social capital, income inequality, and mortality. *American Journal of Public Health, 87*(9), 1491–1498. https://doi.org/10.2105/ajph.87.9.1491

Kawachi, I., Kim, D., Adam, C., & Subramanian, S. V. (2004, August). Commentary: Reconciling the three accounts of social capital. *International Journal of Epidemiology, 33*(4), 682–690. https://doi.org/10.1093/ije/dyh177

Kimmons, R., Veletsianos, G., & Woodward, S. (2017). Institutional uses of Twitter in higher education. *Innovative Higher Education, 42*(1), 97–111.

Klinenberg, E. (2018). *Palaces for the people: How social infrastructure can help fight inequality, polarization, and the decline of civic life.* Crown.

Knack, S., & Keefer, P. (1997). Does social capital have an economic payoff? A cross-country investigation. *Quarterly Journal of Economics, 112*(4), 1251–1288.

Kross, E., Verduyn, P., Demiralp, E., Park, J., Lee, D. S., Lin, N., Shablack, H., Jonides, J., & Ybarra, O. (2013). Facebook use predicts declines in subjective well-being in young adults. *PLoS One, 8*(8), 1–6. https://doi.org/10.1371/journal.pone.0069841

Lomnitz, L. (1977). *Networks and marginality: Life in a Mexican Shanty town.* Academic Press.

Lin, N. (1999). Social networks and status attainment. *Annual Review of Sociology, 25,* 467–487. http://www.jstor.org/stable/223513

Lin, N. (2000). Inequality in social capital. *Contemporary Sociology, 29*(6), 785–795. https://doi.org/10.2307/2654086

Lin, N. (2001). *Social capital: A theory of social structure and action.* Cambridge University Press.

Litt, J. S., Soobader, M. J., Turbin, M. S., Hale, J. W., Buchenau, M., & Marshall, J. A. (2015). The influence of social involvement, neighborhood aesthetics, and community garden participation on fruit and vegetable consumption. *American Journal of Public Health, 105*(3), 443–449.

Liu, C. C. (2008a). Exploring the digital capital of mobile phone service websites by the user's perspective. *International Journal of Mobile Communications, 6*(4), 467. https://doi.org/10.1504/IJMC.2008.018054

Liu, C. C. (2008b). The relationship between digital capital of internet banking and business performance. *International Journal of Electronic Finance, 2*(1), 18. https://doi.org/10.1504/IJEF.2008.016882

Liu, S. B., Komatsu, K., Castaneda-Sanchez, P., & Shirota, S. (2018). A bibliometric review of digital social capital: Mapping a fragmented field. *International Journal of Information Management, 43*, 85–96.

Livingstone, S., & Helsper, E. (2007). Gradations in digital inclusion: Children, young people and the digital divide. *New Media & Society, 9*, 671–696.

Magomedov, M. D., Karabanova, O. V., & Dikikh, V. A. (2020). Digital capital as a basis for the development of the economy in modern time and principles of the digitalization. In *Proceedings of the 2nd international scientific and practical conference on digital economy (ISCDE 2020).* https://doi.org/10.2991/aebmr.k.201205.066

Mayer, R. C., Davis, J. H., & Schoorman, F. D. (1995). An integrative model of organizational trust. *Academy of Management Review, 20*(3), 709–734.

McGillivray, D., & Mahon, J. (2021). Distributed digital capital: Digital literacies and everyday media practices. *Media Practice and Education*, 1–15. https://doi.org/10.1080/25741136.2021.1899628

Merzlikina, G., & Mogharbel, N. (2022). Digital capital as an indicator of the effectiveness of the use of digital technologies in the management of socio-economic systems. *SHS Web of Conferences, 141*, 01011. https://doi.org/10.1051/shsconf/202214101011

Morrow, V. (1999). Conceptualising social capital in relation to the well-being of children and young people: A critical review. *The Sociological Review, 47*(4), 744–765. https://doi.org/10.1111/1467-954X.00194

Nahapiet, J., & Ghoshal, S. (1998). Social capital, intellectual capital, and the organizational advantage. *Academy of Management Review, 23*(2), 242–266.

Park, S. (2017). Understanding digital capital within a user's digital technology ecosystem. In S. Park (Ed.), *Digital capital* (pp. 63–82). Palgrave Macmillan UK. https://doi.org/10.1057/978-1-137-59332-0_4

Pennycook, G., Rand, D. G., & Imas, A. (2018). Imposing social norms via nudges. *Management Science, 67*(11), 4009–4024.

Portes, A. (1998). Social capital: Its origins and applications in modern sociology. *Annual Review of Sociology, 24,* 1–24.

Portes, A., & Sensenbrenner, J. (1993). Embeddedness and immigration: Notes on the social determinants of economic action. *American Journal of Sociology, 98*(6), 1320–1350. http://www.jstor.org/stable/2781823

Preece, J. (2000). *Nurturing social capital in excluded communities a kind of higher education* (ISBN 9781138741461). Taylor and Francis.

Pretty, J., & Ward, H. (2001). Social capital and the environment. *World Development, 29*(2), 209–227.

Putnam, R. D. (1995). Bowling alone: America's declining social capital. *Journal of Democracy, 6*(1), 65–78.

Putnam, R. D. (2000). *Bowling alone: The collapse and revival of American community.* Simon & Schuster.

Ragnedda, M. (2018). Conceptualizing digital capital. *Telematics and Informatics, 35*(8), 2366–2375. https://doi.org/10.1016/j.tele.2018.10.006

Ragnedda, M., & Ruiu, M. L. (2020). *Digital capital.* Emerald. https://doi.org/10.1108/978-1-83909-550-420201002

Resnick, P., Iacovou, N., Suchak, M., Bergstrom, P., & Riedl, J. (2013). Gossip, reputation, and social capital. *ACM Transactions on the Web, 7*(1), 1–33.

Sabatini, F., & Sarracino, F. (2017). Online networks and subjective well-being. *Kyklos, 70*(3), 456–480.

Sadowski, J. (2019). When data is capital: Datafication, accumulation, and extraction. *Big Data & Society, 6*(1). 205395171882054. https://doi.org/10.1177/2053951718820549

Sampson, R. J. (1999). The neighborhood context of well-being. *Perspectives in Biology and Medicine, 46,* S53–S73.

Sanyal, S., & Routray, J. K. (2016). Social capital for disaster risk reduction and management with empirical evidences from Sundarbans of India. *International Journal of Disaster Risk Reduction, 19,* 101–111. ISSN 2212-4209. https://doi.org/10.1016/j.ijdrr.2016.08.010

Scheffler, R. M., Brown, T. T., Syme, L., Kawachi, I., Tolstykh, I., & Iribarren, C. (2008). Community-level social capital and recurrence of acute coronary syndrome. *Social Science & Medicine, 66*(7), 1603–1613.

Schneider, M., Teske, P., Marschall, M., Mintrom, M., & Roch, C. (1997). Institutional arrangements and the creation of social capital: The effects of public school choice. *American Political Science Review*, 91(1), 82–93. https://doi.org/10.2307/2952260

Seale, J. (2013). When digital capital is not enough: Reconsidering the digital lives of disabled university students. *Learning, Media and Technology*, 38(3), 256–269. https://doi.org/10.1080/17439884.2012.670644

Shah, D. V., McLeod, J. M., & Yoon, S. H. (2005). Communication, context, and community: An exploration of print, broadcast, and internet influences. *Communication Theory*, 15(3), 323–347.

Singh, M. K., & Lee, J. (2020). Social inequality and access to social capital in microfinance interventions. *International Journal of Sociology & Social Policy*. ahead-of-p(ahead-of-print). https://doi.org/10.1108/IJSSP-01-2020-0024

Skoric, M. M., Zhu, Q., Goh, D., & Pang, N. (2016). Social media and citizen engagement: A meta-analytic review. *New Media & Society*, 18(9), 1817–1839. https://doi.org/10.1177/1461444815616221

Spitsina, L. Y., Gribanova, E. B., & Spitsin, V. V. (2022). Digital capital of Russian enterprises: Development trends in the digitalisation of the economy and the coronavirus pandemic. *Vestnik Universiteta*, 2, 160–169. https://doi.org/10.26425/1816-4277-2022-2-160-169

Szreter, S., & Woolcock, M. (2004, August). Health by association? Social capital, social theory, and the political economy of public health. *International Journal of Epidemiology*, 33(4), 650–667. https://doi.org/10.1093/ije/dyh013

Tambe, P., Hitt, L., Rock, D., & Brynjolfsson, E. (2020). *Digital capital and superstar firms* (No. w28285, p. w28285). National Bureau of Economic Research. https://doi.org/10.3386/w28285

Tambe, P., Hitt, L. M., Rock, D., & Erik. (2020). *NBER working paper series digital capital and superstar firms.*

Tapscott, D., Lowy, A., & Ticoll, D. (2000). Digital capital: Harnessing the power of business webs. *Thunderbird International Business Review*, 44(1), 5–23.

Tilleczek, K. C., & Campbell, V. M. (Eds.). (2019). *Youth in the digital age: Paradox, promise, predicament* (1st ed.). Routledge. https://doi.org/10.4324/9780429464751

UNICEF. (2020). *C4D gender results.* https://www.unicef.org/india/media/6136/file/C4D-Gender%20Results%20Report.pdf

Uslaner, E. M. (2005). *Coping and social capital: The informal sector and the democratic transition.* https://ssrn.com/abstract=824485; http://doi.org/10.2139/ssrn.824485

Uslaner, E. M. (2002). *The moral foundations of trust.* Cambridge University Press.

Valente, T. W., Pitts, S. R., & An, L. (2015). Social network bridging potential and the use of complementary and alternative medicine in later life. *Journals of Gerontology Series B: Psychological Sciences and Social Sciences, 70*(1), 98–107.

Valenzuela, S., Arriagada, A., & Scherman, A. (2014). The social media basis of youth protest behavior: The case of Chile. *Journal of Communication, 64*(2), 201–223.

Valenzuela, S., Park, N., & Kee, K. F. (2009). Is there social capital in a social network site? Facebook use and college students' life satisfaction, trust, and participation. *Journal of Computer-Mediated Communication, 14*(4), 875–901.

Verba, S., Kay, S., & Henry, B. (1995). *Voice and equality: Civic voluntarism in American politics.* Harvard University Press.

Vitak, J. (2012). The impact of context collapse and privacy on social network site disclosures. *Journal of Broadcasting & Electronic Media, 56*(4), 451–470. https://doi.org/10.1080/08838151.2012.732140

Williams, D. (2006). On and off the 'net: Scales for social capital in an online era. *Journal of Computer-Mediated Communication, 11*, 593–628. https://doi.org/10.1111/j.1083-6101.2006.00029.x

Woolcock, M. (1998). Social capital and economic development: Toward a theoretical synthesis and policy framework. *Theory and Society, 27*, 151–208. https://doi.org/10.1023/A:1006884930135

Woolcock, M. (2001). The place of social capital in understanding social and economic outcomes. *Canadian Journal of Policy Research, 2*(1), 11–17.

Woolcock, M., & Narayan, D. (2000). Social capital: Implications for development theory, research, and policy. *The World Bank Research Observer, 15*(2), 225–249. https://doi.org/10.1093/wbro/15.2.225

Woolcock, M., & Sweetser, A. T. (2002). Bright ideas: Social Capital – The bonds that connect. *ADB Review*, *34*(2).

Word Bank. (2017). *Community and local development program*. https://www.worldbank.org/en/topic/communitydrivendevelopment

World Bank. (2020). *India, women's self-help groups combat the COVID-19 (coronavirus) pandemic*. https://www.worldbank.org/en/news/feature/2020/04/11/women-self-help-groups-combat-covid19-coronavirus-pandemic-india#:~:text=Women's%20self%2Dhelp%20groups%20(SHGs,SHGs%20across%2027%20Indian%20states

Yale University. (2011). *The origins of microfinance: Grameen bank*. Yale School of Management Case Studies. https://vol11.cases.som.yale.edu/kompanion-financial-group/microfinance/origins-microfinance-grameen-bank

Бородкина, О. И., & Сибирев, В. А. (2021). The digital capital of social services consumers: Factors of influence and the need for investment. *The Journal of Social Policy Studies*, *19*(1), 129–142. https://doi.org/10.17323/727-0634-2021-19-1-129-142

MORE SUGGESTED READINGS

Ahn, N., & Kim, Y. (2009). The relationship between social network sites and civic engagement: A case study of Cyworld. *International Journal of Electronic Commerce*, *13*(3), 41–66.

Beugelsdijk, S., & Smulders, S. (2003). *Bridging and bonding social capital: Which type is good for economic growth? The Hague*. CPB.

Burke, M., Marlow, C., & Lento, T. (2010). Social network activity and social well-being. In *Proceedings of the 2010 ACM conference on human factors in computing systems, 1909–1912*.

Caroll, T. F. (2021). *Social capital, land capacity building and poverty reduction*. Asian Development Bank. ISBN 971-561-341-1.

Dasgupta, P. (1996). The economics of social capital. *The Economic Journal*, *106*(436), 1019–1035.

Dwyer, T., Hiltz, S. R., & Passerini, K. (2007). Trust and privacy concerns within social networking sites: A comparison of Facebook and MySpace. *Proceedings of the Thirteenth Americas Conference on Information Systems, 6*.

Faucher, K. X. (2018). *Social capital online: Alienation and accumulation*. University of Westminster Press. https://doi.org/10.16997/book16

Fine, B., & Kinoti, M. (2010). Ethical implications of social capital research. *Journal of Business Ethics*, 96(3), 437–448. This article by Ben Fine and Mary Kinoti explores the ethical implications of social capital research, including concerns related to power dynamics, exclusion, measurement, and context-dependent effects.

Gil de Zúñiga, H., & Chen, H.-T. (2019). Digital media and politics: Effects of the great information and communication divides. *Journal of Broadcasting & Electronic Media*, 63(3), 365–373. https://doi.org/10.1080/08838151.2019.1662019

Hampton, K. N., Lee, C. J., & Her, E. J. (2011). How new media affords network diversity: Direct and mediated access to social capital through participation in local social settings. *New Media & Society*, 13(7), 1031–1049.

Hampton, K. N., & Wellman, B. (2003). Neighboring in Netville: How the Internet supports community and social capital in a wired suburb. *City & Community*, 2(4), 277–311.

Kawachi, I., Kennedy, B. P., & Glass, R. (1999). Social capital and self-rated health: A contextual analysis. *American Journal of Public Health*, 89(8), 1187–1193.

Kim, Y. (2018). Social capital in online communities: A systematic literature review. *Computers in Human Behavior*, 87, 192–206.

Krasnova, H., Wenninger, H., Widjaja, T., & Buxmann, P. (2013). Envy on Facebook: A hidden threat to users' life satisfaction? In *Proceedings of the 11th international conference on Wirtschaftsinformatik* (pp. 1311–1325).

Putnam, R. D. (2001). Bowling alone: The collapse and revival of American community. *Journal of Democracy*, 6(1), 65–78.

Rainie, L., & Wellman, B. (2012). *Networked: The new social operating system*. MIT Press.

Resnick, P. (2002). Beyond bowling together: Sociotechnical capital. In *Proceedings of the 2002 ACM conference on computer supported cooperative work* (pp. 249–258).

Resnick, P., & Montague, R. (2003). Beyond the group mind: Sociotechnical capital. *IBM Systems Journal*, 42(3), 439–443.

Rothstein, B., & Stolle, D. (2003). Social capital, impartiality and the welfare state: An institutional approach. In D. Castiglione, J. van Deth, & G. Wolleb (Eds.), *The handbook of social capital* (pp. 177–198). Oxford University Press.

Ruiu, M. L., & Ragnedda, M. (2020). Digital capital and online activities: An empirical analysis of the second level of digital divide. *First Monday*, *25*(7).

Shirky, C. (2008). *Here comes everybody: The power of organizing without organizations*. Penguin.

Strohmaier, R., Schuetz, M., & Vannuccini, S. (2019). A systemic perspective on socioeconomic transformation in the digital age. *Journal of Industrial and Business Economics*, *46*, 361–378. https://doi.org/10.1007/s40812-019-00124-y

Svendsen, G. T., & Svendsen, G. L. H. (2004). Measuring social capital: The Danish experience. In *Handbook of social capital: The troika of sociology, political science and economics* (pp. 63–88). Edward Elgar Publishing. This book chapter by Gert Tinggaard Svendsen and Gunnar Lind Haase Svendsen discusses the challenges and methods of measuring social capital, including issues related to validity, reliability, and interpretation of social capital data.

Tufekci, Z. (2017). *Twitter and tear gas: The power and fragility of networked protest*. Yale University Press.

van Dijck, J., Poell, T., & de Waal, M. (2018). *The platform society: Public values in a connective world*. Oxford University Press.

Wellman, B. (2001). Physical place and cyberplace: The rise of personalized networking. *International Journal of Urban and Regional Research*, *25*(2), 227–252.

Wellman, B., & Gulia, M. (1999). Virtual communities as communities: Net surfers don't ride alone. In *Networked neighborhoods: The online community in context* (pp. 167–194). Hampton Press.

Zhang, W., Johnson, T. J., Seltzer, T., & Bichard, S. L. (2010). The revolution will be networked: The influence of social networking sites on political attitudes and behavior. *Social Science Computer Review*, *28*(1), 75–92.

INDEX

Printed and bound by CPI Group (UK) Ltd, Croydon, CR0 4YY

24/04/2024

14488195-0002